# STERLING
## Test Prep

# LAW ESSENTIALS

# Contracts

## *Governing Law*

3rd edition

Copyright © 2022 Sterling Test Prep

All rights reserved. This publication's content, including the text and graphic images or part thereof, may not be reproduced, downloaded, disseminated, published, converted to electronic media, or distributed by any means whatsoever without prior written consent from the publisher. Copyright infringement violates federal law and is subject to criminal and civil penalties.

This publication is designed to provide accurate and authoritative information regarding the subject matter covered. It is distributed with the understanding that the publisher, authors, or editors are not engaged in rendering legal or another professional service. If legal advice or other expert assistance is required, a competent professional's services should be sought.

Sterling Test Prep is not legally liable for mistakes, omissions, or inaccuracies in this publication's content. Sterling Test Prep does not guarantee that the user of this publication will pass the bar exam or achieve a performance level. Individual performance depends on many factors, including but not limited to the level of preparation, aptitude, and individual performance on test day.

3  2  1

ISBN-13: 978-1-9547250-8-9

Sterling Test Prep products are available at quantity discounts.

For more information, contact info@sterling–prep.com.

Sterling Test Prep
6 Liberty Square #11
Boston, MA 02109

©2022 Sterling Test Prep

Published by Sterling Test Prep

Printed in the U.S.A.

---

**Customer Satisfaction Guarantee**

Your feedback is important because we strive to provide the highest quality prep materials. Email us comments or suggestions.

info@sterling–prep.com

We reply to emails – check your spam folder

**Thank you for choosing our book!**

# STERLING
## Test Prep

Thousands of students use our study aids to prepare for law school exams and to pass the bar!

Passing the bar is essential for admission to practice law and launching your legal career.

This preparation guide describes the principles of substantive law governing the correct answers to exam questions. It was developed by legal professionals and law instructors who possess extensive credentials and have been admitted to practice law in several jurisdictions. The content is clearly presented and systematically organized for targeted preparation.

The performance on individual questions has been correlated with success or failure on the bar. By analyzing previously administered exams, the authors identified these predictive items and assembled the rules of law that govern the answers to questions tested. Learn the essential governing law to make fine-line distinctions among related principles and decide between tough choices on the exam. This knowledge is vital to excel in law school finals and pass the bar exam.

We look forward to being an essential part of your preparation and wish you great success in the legal profession!

## *Law Essentials* series

Constitutional Law

Contracts

Evidence

Real Property

Torts

Civil Procedure

Criminal Law and Criminal Procedure

Business Associations

Conflict of Laws

Family Law

Secured Transactions

Trusts and Estates

**Visit our Amazon store**

## Comprehensive Glossary of Legal Terms

Over 2,100 essential legal terms defined and explained. An excellent reference source for law students, practitioners and readers seeking an understanding of legal vocabulary and its application.

## Landmark U.S. Supreme Court Cases: Essential Summaries

Learn important constitutional cases that shaped American law. Understand how the evolving needs of society intersect with the U.S. Constitution. Short summaries of seminal Supreme Court cases focused on issues and holdings.

**Visit our Amazon store**

## Table of Contents

**CONTRACTS GOVERNING LAW** ............................................................... 13

**Contract Law – Overview** ........................................................................ 15
    Definition of and parties to a contract ................................................ 15
    Requirements of a contract .................................................................. 15
    Capacity to contract ............................................................................. 16
    The Statute of Frauds – writing requirement ...................................... 17
    Fraud ..................................................................................................... 17

**Formation of Contracts** ............................................................................ 19
    Offer ...................................................................................................... 19
    Acceptance ............................................................................................ 19
    Revocation of offers ............................................................................. 21
    Rejection ............................................................................................... 22
    Mistake, fraud and duress .................................................................... 23
    Indefiniteness and absence of terms .................................................... 23
    Capacity to contract ............................................................................. 23
    Implied-in-fact contracts ...................................................................... 24
    Implied-in-law contracts ...................................................................... 24
    Quasi-contracts ..................................................................................... 24
    Pre-contractual liability based upon detrimental reliance ................... 24
    Unconscionability ................................................................................ 25

**Consideration** ............................................................................................ 27
    Bargain and exchange ......................................................................... 27
    Adequacy of consideration .................................................................. 27
    Detrimental reliance ............................................................................. 28
    Moral obligations ................................................................................. 28
    Modification of contracts and pre-existing duty rule .......................... 28
    Compromise and settlement of claims ................................................ 29
    Output and requirements contracts ...................................................... 29

**Third-Party Beneficiary Contracts** ........................................................ 31
    Intended beneficiaries .......................................................................... 31
    Incidental beneficiaries ........................................................................ 32
    Modification of the third-party beneficiary's rights ............................ 32

**Assignment and Delegation** ..................................................................... 33
    Assignment of rights ............................................................................ 33
    Delegation of duties ............................................................................. 33

## CONTRACTS GOVERNING LAW (*continued*)

### Statute of Frauds ... 35
- Memorandum ... 35
- Contract cannot be performed within one year ... 35
- Land contracts ... 35
- General rule for the sale of goods ... 35
- Exceptions for sale of goods ... 36
- Suretyship ... 36

### Parol Evidence Rule ... 39
- Exceptions to the parol evidence rule ... 39

### Interpretation of Contracts ... 41
- Employment-at-will ... 41
- UCC course of dealing and usage of trade ... 41

### Conditions ... 43
- Express conditions ... 43
- Constructive conditions of exchange ... 43
- Divisible contracts ... 44
- Immaterial breach and substantial performance ... 44
- Installment contracts ... 45
- UCC rule – implied warranty of merchantability ... 45
- UCC rule – warranty of fitness for a particular purpose ... 45
- Constructive condition of cooperation ... 46
- Obligations of good faith and fair dealing ... 46
- Suspension or excuse of conditions by waiver ... 46

### Remedies ... 47
- Rescission ... 47
- Buyer's and seller's obligations unless terms are specified ... 47
- Cure ... 47
- Rights of the non-breaching party ... 47
- Demand for assurances ... 47
- Anticipatory repudiation ... 48
- Risk of loss ... 48
- Rights of *bona fide* purchasers ... 49
- Seller's remedies in the event of buyer's breach ... 49
- Buyer's remedies in the event of seller's breach ... 49
- Measure of damages ... 49
- Consequential damages ... 50

## CONTRACTS GOVERNING LAW (*continued*)

### Remedies (*continued*)
Liquidated damages ... 50
Specific performance ... 51
Restitution damages (*quantum meruit*) ... 51

### Monetary Damages for Breach of Contract Actions ... 53

### Impossibility and Frustration ... 55
Impossibility of performance ... 55
Excused performance under the UCC ... 55

### Conflict of Laws in Contracts ... 57
Place of contracting ... 57
Special rules ... 58
Place of performance for other issues ... 58
Applying choice-of-law rules to specific issues ... 59

### Establishing Agency ... 61

### Contracts – Quick Facts ... 63

### Review Questions ... 67
Multiple-choice questions ... 67
True/false questions ... 70
Answer keys ... 72

## EXAM INFORMATION, PREPARATION AND TEST-TAKING STRATEGIES ... 73

### Introduction to the Uniform Bar Examination (UBE) ... 75
Structure of the UBE ... 75
The Multistate Bar Examination (MBE) ... 75
Interpreting the UBE score report ... 75
The importance of the MBE score ... 76
MEE and MPT scores ... 77
The objective of the Multistate Bar Exam ... 77

### Preparation Strategies for the Bar Exam ... 79
An effective bar exam study schedule and plan ... 79
Focused studying ... 80
Advice on using outlines ... 80
Easy questions make the difference ... 81
Study plan based upon statistics ... 82
Factors associated with passing the bar ... 82
Pass rates based on GPA and LSAT scores ... 83

## EXAM INFORMATION, PREP & TEST-TAKING STRATEGIES (*continued*)

### Learning and Applying the Substantive Law ............................................. 85
- Knowledge of substantive law ............................................. 85
- Where to find the law ............................................. 86
- Controlling authority ............................................. 86
- Recent changes in the law ............................................. 87
- Lesser-known issues and unusual applications ............................................. 87
- Practice applying the governing law ............................................. 87
- Know which governing law is being tested ............................................. 88
- Answers which are always wrong ............................................. 88

### Honing Reading Skills ............................................. 89
- Understanding complex transactions ............................................. 89
- Impediments to careful reading ............................................. 89
- Reading too much into a question ............................................. 89
- Read the call of the question first ............................................. 90
- Negative calls ............................................. 90
- Read all choices ............................................. 90
- Broad statements of black letter law may be correct ............................................. 90

### Multiple-Choice Test-Taking Tactics ............................................. 91
- Determine the single correct answer ............................................. 91
- Process of elimination ............................................. 91
- Elimination increases the odds ............................................. 91
- Eliminating two wrong answers ............................................. 92
- Pick the winning side ............................................. 92
- Distance between choices on the other side ............................................. 92
- Questions based upon a common fact pattern ............................................. 93
- Multiple true/false issues ............................................. 93
- Correctly stated, but the inapplicable principle of law ............................................. 93
- "Because" questions ............................................. 94
- "If" questions ............................................. 94
- "Because" or "if" need not be exclusive ............................................. 94
- Exam tip for "because" ............................................. 94
- "Only if" requires exclusivity ............................................. 95
- "Unless" questions ............................................. 95
- Limiting words ............................................. 95

## EXAM INFORMATION, PREP & TEST-TAKING STRATEGIES (continued)

**Making Correct Judgment Calls** ............................................................. 97
    Applying the law to the facts ............................................................. 97
    Bad judgment equals the wrong answer ............................................. 97
    Judgment calls happen ...................................................................... 97
    The importance of procedure ............................................................. 98

**Exam Tips and Suggestions** .................................................................... 99
    Timing is everything ........................................................................... 99
    An approach for when time is not an issue ........................................ 99
    An approach for when time is an issue ............................................. 100
    Difficult questions ............................................................................. 100
    Minimize fatigue to maximize your score ......................................... 100
    Proofread the answer sheet ............................................................. 101
    Intelligent preparation over a sustained period ................................ 101

**Essay Preparation Strategies and Essay-Writing Suggestions** ................ 103
    Memorize the law ............................................................................ 103
    Focus on the highly tested essay rules ............................................. 103
    Practice writing essay answers each week ...................................... 103
    Add one essay-specific subject each week ...................................... 103

**Essay Preparation Strategies and Essay-Writing Suggestions** (continued)
    Make it easy for the grader to award points .................................... 104
    Conclusion for each essay question .................................................. 104
    Tips for an easy-to-read essay .......................................................... 105
    Think before you write .................................................................... 105
    The ability to think and communicate like a lawyer ......................... 105
    Do not restate the facts ................................................................... 106
    Do not state abstract or irrelevant propositions of law .................... 106
    Discuss all the issues raised ............................................................. 107
    Methods for finding all issues .......................................................... 107
    Indicators requiring alternative arguments ...................................... 107
    Avoid ambiguous, rambling statements and verbosity ..................... 108
    Avoid undue repetition .................................................................... 108
    Avoid slang and colloquialism .......................................................... 108
    Write legibly and coherently ............................................................ 108
    Timing strategies .............................................................................. 109
    Stay focused .................................................................................... 109
    Law school essay grading matrix ..................................................... 109

## APPENDIX ............................................................................................................111

### Overview of American Law (*diagram*) .................................................................113

### U.S. Court Systems – Federal and State Courts ..................................................115
Jurisdiction of federal and state courts ...............................................................115
Organization of the federal courts ......................................................................117

### How Civil Cases Move Through the Federal Courts ..........................................119
Jury trials ............................................................................................................119
Bench trials .........................................................................................................120
Jury selection ......................................................................................................120
Instructions and standard of proof .....................................................................120
Judgment ............................................................................................................121
Right to appeal ...................................................................................................121

### How Criminal Cases Move Through the Federal Courts ..................................123
Indictment or information ..................................................................................123
Arraignment .......................................................................................................124
Investigation .......................................................................................................124
Deliberation and verdict ....................................................................................124
Judgment and sentencing ..................................................................................125
Right to appeal ..................................................................................................125

### How Civil and Criminal Appeals Move Through the Federal Courts ...............127
Assignment of judges .........................................................................................127
Review of a lower court decision .......................................................................127
Oral argument ....................................................................................................127
Decision .............................................................................................................127
The Supreme Court of the United States ..........................................................128

### Standards of Review for Federal Courts (*table*) .................................................130

### The Constitution of the United States (*a transcription*) ....................................131
Preamble ............................................................................................................131
Article I ..............................................................................................................131
Article II .............................................................................................................136
Article III ...........................................................................................................138
Article IV ...........................................................................................................139
Article V ............................................................................................................139
Article VI ..........................................................................................................140
Article VII .........................................................................................................140

**APPENDIX** (*continued*)

    **Enactment of the Bill of Rights of the United States of America (1791)** ............... 141

    **The Bill of Rights: Amendments I–X** ............... 143

    **Constitutional Amendments XI–XXVII** ............... 145

        Amendment XI ............... 145

        Amendment XII ............... 145

        Amendment XIII ............... 146

        Amendment XIV ............... 146

        Amendment XV ............... 147

        Amendment XVI ............... 147

        Amendment XVII ............... 147

        Amendment XVIII ............... 148

        Amendment XIX ............... 148

        Amendment XX ............... 148

        Amendment XXI ............... 149

        Amendment XXII ............... 150

        Amendment XXIII ............... 150

        Amendment XXIV ............... 150

        Amendment XXV ............... 151

        Amendment XXVI ............... 152

        Amendment XXII ............... 152

    **States' Rights Under the U.S. Constitution** ............... 153

        Selective incorporation under the 14$^{th}$ Amendment ............... 153

        Federalism in the United States ............... 153

# Contracts Governing Law

Contracts is a stand-alone topic testing common law principles and the sales of goods (UCC Article 2). To maximize your score, focus on the frequently tested topics of contract formation, performance, breach, discharge of obligations, contract enforceability, third-party rights, parol evidence, interpretation, damages, and contract remedies.

The statements herein were compiled by analyzing released Contracts questions and setting forth the principles of law governing the correct answers. Review these principles before preparing answers to practice Contracts questions. Memorize this governing law and understand how it applies to the correct answer.

Per the National Conference of Bar Examiners (NCBE), assume the Official Text of Articles 1 and 2 of the Uniform Commercial Code (UCC) has been adopted.

## Contract Law – Overview

### Definition of and parties to a contract

A *contract* is an agreement that is enforceable by a court of law or equity.

*Second Restatement on Contracts*: a contract is a promise or a set of promises for the breach of which the law gives a remedy or the performance of which the law recognizes a duty.

Parties to a contract:

> *Offeror* – the party who makes an offer.

> *Offeree* – the party to whom the offer is made.

### Requirements of a contract

To be an enforceable contract, the following four basic requirements must be met:

- Agreement – there must be an agreement between the parties.
- Consideration – a *bargained-for* consideration must support the promise.
- Contractual capacity – the parties must have the capacity to contract.
- Lawful object – the object of the contract must be lawful.

*Agreement* is the manifestation by persons of the contract's substance.

> *Acceptance* is the *manifestation of assent* by the offeree to the terms of the offer.

> Acceptance of the offer creates a contract.

*Consideration* is the thing of value given in exchange for a promise.

> Gift or gratuitous promises are unenforceable because they lack consideration.

> An *illusory promise* is not enforceable due to a lack of consideration. For example, a promise *to paint a house if time permits*.

*Contractual capacity* – parties must have mental capacity to be bound by a contract.

*Lawful object*. The object of the contract must be lawful. A contract to perform an illegal act is void.

> Contracts contrary to public policy are illegal (e.g., murder, theft).

*Requirements of the offer*

> The offeror must objectively intend to be bound by the offer.

> The terms of the offer must be definite or reasonably certain.

The offer must be communicated to the offeree.

*Termination of the offer*

A counteroffer simultaneously terminates the offer and creates a new offer.

A contract may be either express or implied.

*Express contracts* are stated in oral or written words.

*Implied-in-fact contracts* are implied from the conduct of the parties.

*Executed contract* has promises made and completed immediately (e.g., product purchase at a store).

*Executory contract* has promises made but not entirely performed immediately (e.g., apartment lease, painting contract).

## Capacity to contract

The law presumes that the parties to a contract have the requisite contractual capacity.

Minors do not always have the maturity, experience, or sophistication needed to enter into contracts with adults.

The infancy doctrine allows minors to disaffirm most contracts with adults.

The minor has the option of choosing whether to enforce the contract.

The contract is voidable by a minor.

Minors are obligated to pay for the necessities of life for which they contract.

Mentally incompetent persons

The law protects people suffering from mental incapacity from enforcing contracts against them.

Intoxicated persons

Most states provide that contracts entered into by intoxicated persons are *voidable* by that person.

## The Statute of Frauds – writing requirement

All states have enacted a Statute of Frauds.

Generally, for contracts covered by the Statute of Frauds, an executory contract not in writing is not enforceable.

Contracts must be in writing to be enforceable under the Statute of Frauds (see discussion elsewhere).

Contracts requiring a writing:

1) Land contracts – transfers of ownership interests in real property must be in writing.

2) One-year rule – contracts that cannot be completed within a year (assuming unlimited money and human resources). For example, singing at a person's birthday party in 18 months from contract formation

3) Contracts for the Sales of Goods over $500.

4) Contracts to be responsible as a surety for another's debts.

5) Contracts in consideration of marriage.

6) Contracts by the executor of a will to pay a debt of the estate from their monies.

The formality of the writing requires a signature.

## Fraud

Material Misrepresentation of Fact

Intent to deceive

Reliance on the misrepresentation

Injury to the innocent party

*Notes for active learning*

## Formation of Contracts

### Offer

To form a contract, there must be an offer that is accepted.

A person makes an "offer" to enter into a bilateral contract by communicating to another person a proposed exchange of promises between the parties. The recipient of the communication reasonably believes that they can enter into a binding contract by accepting that proposed exchange of promises.

The more precise the communication, the more likely it will be characterized as an offer.

Communication is an offer for a unilateral contract if it sets forth valid consideration in exchange for a proposed action by the addressee, in such a manner that the person to whom it is directed reasonably believes that they can enter into a binding contract by performing the requested action.

**UCC rule:** A sale of goods contract may be made in a manner sufficient to show agreement even though the moment of its making is undetermined.

### Acceptance

While rules govern how an offer is accepted in the absence of specific conditions of acceptance set forth in the offer, the offeror has a right to specify the manner of acceptance and make the usual rules inoperative.

If the offeror does not specify conditions for acceptance, an offer may be accepted at a reasonable time and in a reasonable manner.

If the offer is one for a unilateral contract, it may be accepted only by the performance of the act requested, not by a return promise.

Unless the parties have had a course of dealing where the offeree has accepted offers from the offeror by doing nothing, an offeror will be unsuccessful in arguing that silence by the offeree constitutes acceptance.

Unless the terms of an offer or course of dealing permit the offeree to accept by doing nothing, an offeree will be unsuccessful in arguing that they accepted an offer by silence.

For contracts controlled by common law and not the UCC (i.e., common law contracts), the offeree can only accept an offer by communicating acceptance of the terms of the offer before the time the offer expires, is terminated, or revoked.

Unless the offeror requires a different acceptance method in the offer, an offer is accepted when the letter of acceptance is mailed.

Words of the offeree which the offeror can reasonably believe an acceptance will cause a contract to be formed, even if those words do not include the term "accept."

**UCC rules:** Under § 2-206, an offer to buy goods for prompt shipment is accepted when the seller ships the goods, and a binding contract is formed at that time.

Unless otherwise unambiguously indicated by the language or circumstances,

(a) an offer to make a contract shall be construed as inviting acceptance in any manner and by any medium reasonable in the circumstances, and,

(b) an order or another offer to buy goods for prompt or current shipment shall be construed as inviting acceptance, either by a prompt promise to ship or by the prompt or current shipment of conforming or non-conforming goods.

Such a shipment of non-conforming goods does not constitute an acceptance if the seller reasonably notifies the buyer that the shipment is offered only as an accommodation.

Where the beginning of a requested performance is a reasonable mode of acceptance, an offeror who is not notified of acceptance within a reasonable time may treat the offer as having lapsed before acceptance.

**UCC rules:** Under § 2-207(1), a definite and reasonable expression of acceptance or a written confirmation sent within a reasonable time operates as an acceptance even though it states terms additional to or different from those offered or agreed upon unless acceptance is expressly made conditional on assent to the additional or different terms.

Under § 2-207(2), the additional terms are to be construed as proposals for an addition to the contract.

Between merchants, such terms become part of the contract unless:

(a) the offer expressly limits acceptance to the terms of the offer,

(b) the additional terms materially alter the offer, or

(c) notification of objection to the terms is given within a reasonable time after notice of them is received.

If the proposed additional term materially changes the original offer, there is still a contract, but the additional term is not included.

Under § 2-207(3), conduct by both parties, which recognizes the existence of a contract is sufficient to establish a contract for sale. The writings of the parties do not otherwise establish a contract.

The terms of the contract consist of those terms on which the writings of the parties agree, with supplementary terms incorporated under any other provisions of this Act.

If a seller under the UCC ships non-conforming goods in response to an offer and indicates that they have not accepted the original offer, the shipment of the non-conforming goods is a counteroffer. The seller is not in breach of contract for shipping the non-conforming goods.

If the buyer accepts the non-conforming goods and the counteroffer, they must pay the full contract price.

### Revocation of offers

At common law, an offer is revocable by the offeror at any time, even if the offeror promises to keep the offer open for some time.

At common law, an offer is irrevocable if the agreement to keep it open for a specified period is supported by consideration.

Such an offer is an option contract.

The offeror may not revoke an offer for a unilateral contract if the offeror knows that the offeree has commenced substantial performance.

To be effective, the revocation must be communicated to the offeree before the offeree accepts the offer.

A revocation need not be in the express language.

Any communication, such as "I have sold it to someone else," which reasonably indicates to the offeree that the offer has been withdrawn, is a revocation.

A revocation need not be a direct communication between the offeror and the offeree.

If the offeree learns from a third party that the offer has been revoked before the offeree has accepted the offer, the revocation is effective.

An offer for a unilateral contract which occurs when the owner of real estate hires a broker and agrees to pay a commission when and if the broker finds a buyer ready, willing, and able to purchase the property, is automatically revoked without notice if the owner accepts another offer to purchase the property.

A written offer required by the Statute of Frauds can be revoked orally.

The death of the offeror terminates an offer.

If a contract has been formed, either party's death does not terminate the contract unless a party's death makes the contract impossible to perform.

**UCC rules:** A "merchant" means a person who deals in goods of the kind, or otherwise by their occupation holds themself out as having knowledge or skill peculiar to the practices or goods involved in the transaction, or to whom such knowledge or skill may be attributed by their employment of an agent, broker, or another intermediary who by occupation holds themself out as having knowledge or skill.

"Between merchants" means a transaction for which both parties are chargeable with the knowledge or skill of merchants.

An offer by a merchant to buy or sell goods in a signed writing, which by its terms gives assurances that it will be held open, is not revocable, for lack of consideration, during the time stated, or, if no time is stated, for a reasonable time.

In no event may such period of irrevocability exceed three months.

The offeror must separately sign a term of assurance on a form supplied by the offeree.

An offer by a non-merchant for the sale of goods under the UCC is revocable in the same manner as an offer at common law.

An oral offer by a merchant for the sale of goods is revocable in the same manner as an offer at common law.

A merchant's written offer, which states that the offer remains open for more than three months, remains irrevocable for three months.

## Rejection

If at common law, the offeree purports to accept an offer but changes the terms of the offer in any way, the communication is a counteroffer, and no contract is formed.

This rule is qualified for the sale of goods by § 2-207 discussed above.

An offer is terminated by rejection or by a counteroffer. After that, the offeree cannot accept the original offer even if the time to remain open has not expired.

If the offeror has made a multipart offer that can be accepted in part, such as "I will sell you any one of these five lots for $5,000 apiece," acceptance of part of the offer can be considered as a rejection of the remainder of the offer.

An inquiry concerning the offer by the offeree about the offeror's precise terms or willingness of the offeror to modify the terms of the offer is not a rejection.

## Mistake, fraud and duress

The defense of unilateral mistake is available when one party's mistake was so apparent that the other party should have known the mistake when the offer was accepted.

Unilateral mistake is grounds for avoiding a contract if the first party is mistaken about a material fact. While not mistaken about that fact, the second party is aware that the first party is mistaken about that material fact.

Mutual mistake is grounds for avoiding a contract if both parties relied on an untrue material fact at the time of contracting.

There is no meeting of the minds, an essential requirement for a contract's existence if each party to the contract without fault has a different understanding of the meaning of the words they agreed to.

If the contract involves the ship "Peerless," but each party innocently and honestly thinks of a different ship named "Peerless," there is no meeting of the minds and no contract.

If the parties orally agree on terms of a contract, which is reduced to writing and the scrivener makes an error in setting out the terms of the contract, either party can reform the written contract to conform to the actual oral understanding of the parties.

## Indefiniteness and absence of terms

**UCC rule:** A contract is not void for indefiniteness if there is no price agreed to. Under UCC, there is a valid contract for a reasonable price.

## Capacity to contract

A person who has entered into a contract while a minor can disaffirm that contract, even one that has been completed, except a contract for necessities, within a reasonable time of reaching the age of majority.

If a minor, after reaching majority, agrees to make a payment on a contract they had a right to disaffirm, for an amount which is less than the full contract price, the agreement is only enforceable without new consideration to the extent of the promise made after reaching majority, not for the full contract price.

## Implied-in-fact contracts

An implied-in-fact contract arises out of the conscious action of a party.

Without words spoken or written, a contractual obligation can be implied from a party's action. For example, accepting services from someone in providing those services creates an obligation to pay those services' fair value.

If a landowner watches another party perform work on their land, which they know is not intended to be gratuitous and says nothing, the landowner has entered into an implied-in-fact contract to pay for the fair value of the work.

## Implied-in-law contracts

An implied-in-law contract arises even though a party has not acted in word or deed to incur contractual liability.

The law will imply a contractual liability to pay for necessary services rendered to an individual when they lack the mental capacity to request such services or agree to be contractually bound to pay.

## Quasi-contracts

If parties entered or attempted to enter into a contractual relationship, but the contract is not enforceable because of the Statute of Frauds or other reasons, and one party conferred a benefit on the other, the party conferring the benefit can sue in quasi-contract for the fair value of the benefit conferred. Contract measures of damages do not apply.

A person who has a right to pursue a remedy under an enforceable contract does not have the right to sue in *quantum meruit* (i.e., a reasonable sum of money) for a benefit conferred.

## Pre-contractual liability based upon detrimental reliance

If the owner of property puts a construction contract out to bid to general contractors, and a subcontractor submits an offer to perform a subcontract for the general contractor, with the knowledge that the general contractor is relying on the bid when bidding for the general contract, the subcontract's bid is treated as an option contract.

The general contractor's detrimental reliance is a sufficient substitute for bargained-for consideration so that the subcontractor cannot revoke their bid. The general contractor has a reasonable time after they become the successful bidder to accept the bid.

However, since the subcontractor's bid is an offer, there is no contract between the general contractor and the subcontractor until the general contractor accepts the bid.

## Unconscionability

Unconscionability arises when there are unfair terms coupled with an unfair bargaining process.

A contract is unconscionable, and a court can refuse to enforce such a contract if one of its provisions was oppressive at the time of the contract's execution.

The concept of unconscionable is part of the UCC and applied with increasing frequency to common law contracts.

*Notes for active learning*

## Consideration

### Bargain and exchange

The concept of the bargain is the essence of consideration.

A promise by one party to perform an act or refrain from acting, in exchange for a counter-promise by the other party to perform an act or refrain from acting, constitutes valid consideration, making the promises enforceable.

For valid consideration, the party making the bargain need not be the person benefiting.

An agreement is supported by consideration if the person benefited is a third party for whom the benefit was requested.

If a party promises to do something that they are not legally obligated to, they have given consideration even though the performance of that obligation is not burdensome.

A promise that does not limit a party's rights is an *illusory promise* that does not constitute valid consideration because the promisor possesses a unilateral right to avoid an obligation made in the promise.

"I promise to pay you one dollar for that apple if I choose to" is an illusory promise.

If a promise is illusory because its enforceability is subject to a condition precedent that is entirely within one party's control, a valid contract forms once the condition is satisfied.

The promise to undertake a minor burden imposed on the recipient of property in what is essentially a donative transaction does not transform that burden into consideration.

For example, an aunt's statement to her nephew, "I will buy you a jacket for your birthday if you stop by the store to pick it up," creates a donative transaction because the aunt is not bargaining with her nephew about picking up the jacket.

### Adequacy of consideration

In determining whether a contract is supported by consideration, courts do not measure the value of what a party promises compared to what they receive.

An agreement to settle a meritless claim is not valid consideration.

Suppose an agreement is supported by consideration so that a valid contract exists. According to its terms, a party who performs their side of the bargain is entitled to enforce the contract even if they get far more than given.

## Detrimental reliance

Even if an agreement is not supported by bargained-for consideration, such as a promise to make a gift, it may be enforceable if there is a substitute for bargained-for consideration; promissory estoppel.

If an agreement is supported by bargained-for consideration, the promissory estoppel elements are irrelevant and the wrong answer to a multiple-choice question.

An agreement not supported by bargained-for consideration, such as a promise to make a gift, is enforceable if promissory estoppel (the substitute for bargained-for consideration) is present.

Promissory estoppel is present if:

1) one party knows that their promise induces substantial reliance by the promisee, and

2) failure to enforce the promise causes substantial hardship, and

3) injustice can be avoided only by such enforcement.

## Moral obligations

A service that has already been gratuitously rendered is not valid consideration for a later promise to pay because the bargain element (i.e., the essence of consideration) is absent.

Even though there is no new bargain, a unilateral promise in writing to pay a debt barred by the statute of limitations (SOL) is enforceable without new consideration.

If the new promise differs from the original, the contract is only enforceable to the extent of the new promise.

A contract that was initially voidable because of age is enforceable against that party without new consideration if the minor makes a new promise after reaching majority.

If the new promise differs from the original promise, the contract is only enforceable to the extent of the new promise.

## Modification of contracts and pre-existing duty rule

An agreement to rescind an existing executory contract is supported by consideration since each side is bargaining to give up the rights they previously had under the contract.

The common-law rule is that fresh consideration (a different obligation than already agreed to) must support contract modification. The agreement to modify is unenforceable if one party's promises are unmodified and the other party's promises are more burdensome.

A contract can be modified at common law if each gives new consideration for modification.

Consideration is not an issue if one party to an existing contract modifies its promises in exchange for the other party's promise to modify its promises.

Modern common law contract cases hold that an agreement to modify an existing contract without fresh consideration is enforceable when the modification is made in good faith. An example of good faith is when the circumstances under which the contract is to be performed changed through no fault of the parties when the contract was executed.

The traditional common-law rule was that if a party to a contract agreed with the other party to perform an act that they were already obligated to perform because of contractual relations with a third person, the agreement was unenforceable as not supported by consideration.

Under modern contract principles tested, the contractual obligation to a third party to perform the act does not prevent the promise to perform the act from being adequate consideration.

**UCC rule:** An agreement modifying a contract needs no new consideration to be binding.

### Compromise and settlement of claims

Forbearance, a promise not to assert a right, is not valid consideration if the agreement forbears asserting a frivolous claim that the party knows is invalid.

Forbearance is valid consideration if the person seeking to enforce the contract reasonably believes that they have a valid legal claim.

When there is a dispute concerning the amount owed, and one party tenders a check as payment in full, which the other party cashes, there is a discharge of the contractual obligation.

If the claim's amount and validity are undisputed, the cashing of the check does not bar a suit for the remainder.

If there is no dispute concerning either the validity, collectability, or amount of the claim, an agreement to settle the claim for a lower amount is not supported by consideration.

### Output and requirements contracts

Output and requirements contracts are not invalid on the grounds of indefiniteness or lack of consideration.

Output and requirements contracts are specifically enforceable if the non-breaching party will have difficulty obtaining substitute performance.

**UCC rules:** A quantity term expressed as a manufacturer's requirements is enforceable.

UCC § 2-306 provides that "a term which measures the quantity by the . . . requirements of the buyer mean such actual . . . requirements as may occur in good faith . . ."

The definiteness of quantity requirement is satisfied if there is an available objective method for determining the quantity, and the requirements of a manufacturer would generally satisfy that need.

No quantity unreasonably disproportionate to any stated estimate, or in the absence of a stated estimate, to a standard or otherwise comparable prior output or requirements, may be tendered or demanded.

A lawful agreement by either the seller or the buyer for exclusive dealing in the kind of goods concerned imposes, unless otherwise agreed, an obligation by the seller to use best efforts to supply the goods and the buyer to use best efforts to promote their sale.

## Third-Party Beneficiary Contracts

### Intended beneficiaries

Third-party beneficiary contracts arise when the performance of one of the parties' contractual obligations benefits a person, not a party to the contract, instead of the party who furnished the consideration necessary for that obligation to arise.

Thus "A" and "B" enter into a contract whereby A furnishes consideration to B, who is contractually obligated to render performance to "C," not A.

If two parties contract a service that each intends to benefit a designated third party, the third-party beneficiary and promisee are entitled to sue upon the promisor's breach.

The victim of a breach is entitled to recover only those damages which could not reasonably have been avoided.

Failure to take reasonable steps to mitigate damages defeats a claim for consequential damages.

No contractual rights vest in an intended third-party beneficiary unless the promisor and promisee parties conclude a binding contract.

Third-party beneficiaries are intended beneficiaries when the contracting parties either explicitly or implicitly direct the contract's performance for their benefit.

A *creditor beneficiary* is a type of intended beneficiary where the contract's performance for the benefit of the beneficiary, C, is designed to relieve the party who furnished the consideration, A, from a legal obligation.

A *donee beneficiary* is another type of intended third-party beneficiary where the original contracting party, A, satisfies no legal obligation by entering into a contract designed to benefit C.

Since one of the contracting parties, A, has furnished the consideration which obligated B to perform, the third party, C, need not provide consideration to be able to sue on a third-party beneficiary contract.

A third-party creditor beneficiary, C, does not give up their rights against the contracting party who furnished the consideration, A, which required that performance be rendered to them until the party obligated to render performance, B, completes their obligation.

Intended third-party beneficiaries need not know that a contract has been made for their benefit when they become a third-party beneficiary to have the right to sue.

If a party to a third party beneficiary contract, B, is obligated to render performance to an intended third-party beneficiary, C, in exchange for performance by A., they are relieved of that obligation if A does not perform their obligations to B.

Therefore, B has a valid defense in a suit by C if A fails to perform its obligations to B.

### Incidental beneficiaries

An incidental beneficiary, a person benefited if a contract between two other parties is performed but is a person that the original contracting parties did not intend to benefit, has no right to enforce a third-party beneficiary contract.

### Modification of the third-party beneficiary's rights

The two original parties to a third-party beneficiary contract, A and B, can modify or rescind their contract to the detriment of the intended beneficiary, C, up until the time that C's rights in the contract become vested.

They become vested when C either assents to the contract at a party's request, sues on the contract, or changes position in reliance on it.

## Assignment and Delegation

### Assignment of rights

An assignee succeeds in a contract as the contract stands at the time of assignment.

Once a party has fully performed obligations under a contract, their right to return performance, including the right to sue for breach of the other party's obligations, can be assigned to a third party even if the contract prohibits assignment.

A party to a contract can assign the benefits of the contract, which accrue without obligating the assignee to assume the burdens of the contract.

An assignee of a contract only obtains rights under it, which are limited by defenses that the original contracting party has against the assignor.

The rule is contrary to the rule when the assignment is a negotiable instrument.

The assignee, known as a *holder in due course*, takes free of the personal defenses that the other party to the negotiable instrument has against the instrument's assignor.

If a contracting party pays a second contracting party an amount due on the contract before receiving notice that the second party assigned their interest under the contract, the first party is not obligated to an assignee, even though the assignment took place before the payment.

If the first party has been notified of the assignment before making payment, they can only discharge their contract obligation by paying the assignee.

**UCC rule:** Unless otherwise agreed, all rights of either seller or buyer can be assigned except where the assignment would materially change the duty of the other party, increase materially the burden or risk imposed by contract, or impair their chances of obtaining return performance materially.

Unless the circumstances indicate the contrary, a prohibition of the contract assignment is to be construed as barring only the delegation to the assignee of the assignor's performance.

### Delegation of duties

A contractual provision forbidding delegation is valid and enforceable.

A party may perform their duty through a delegatee unless:

1) it is otherwise agreed, or

2) the other party has a substantial interest in having the original promisor perform, or

3) the party wishing to delegate possesses unique characteristics (e.g., a singer), so the performance by a delegatee materially alters the bargained-for performance.

No delegation of performance relieves the party delegating duty to perform or liability for breach.

If the parties enter into a novation so that one original contracting party agrees to look solely to the delegatee for performance in exchange for releasing the other original party from the contract's obligations, the original party is no longer liable if the delegatee breaches the contract.

**UCC rule:** An assignment of "the contract" or "all my rights under the contract" or an assignment in similarly general terms is an assignment of rights and duties.

Unless the language or the circumstances (e.g., an assignment for security) indicate to the contrary, it is a delegation of the duties of the assignor's performance.

The acceptance of the assignee's assignment constitutes a promise to perform those duties.

The promise is enforceable by the assignor or the other party to the original contract.

## Statute of Frauds

The exemption of contracts for less than $500 from the Statute of Frauds requirements applies only to contracts for the sale of goods governed by UCC-2.

### Memorandum

The Statute of Frauds applies to specific types of contracts discussed below. The contract itself need not be in writing to satisfy the statute.

There need only be a memorandum that contains the essential terms of the contract signed by the party to be charged.

The memorandum sufficient to satisfy the statute need not be written when making the promise, nor need it to be writing addressed to the promisee.

### Contract cannot be performed within one year

In measuring the one year to determine if the Statute of Frauds is applicable, the period starts when making the contract, not at the commencement of performance.

The Statute of Frauds applies to an eleven-month personal services contract made on January 1 with work starting on April 1, since the contract will not terminate until March 1 of the following year.

The possibility that death could prematurely terminate a personal services contract for more than a year does not cause the Statute of Frauds to be inapplicable.

The Statute of Frauds does not apply to a personal services contract for the life of the party because the natural termination of that contract could occur within a year.

### Land contracts

See Property Law for the Statute of Frauds as it applies to land contracts.

A real estate brokerage contract is enforceable even if there is no memorandum signed by the property owner sufficient to satisfy the Statute of Frauds.

### General rule for the sale of goods

**UCC rules:** Except as otherwise provided, a contract for the sale of goods for the price of $500 or more is not enforceable by action or defense unless there is a writing sufficient to indicate that a contract for sale had been made between the parties.

This writing must be signed by the party against whom enforcement is sought or by their authorized agent or broker.

A writing is not insufficient because it omits or incorrectly states a term agreed upon, but the contract is not enforceable beyond the number of goods shown in such writing.

A memorandum satisfies the Statute of Frauds if it indicates a contract; it contains a description of the goods, quantity and is signed. It does not need to contain the price.

### Exceptions for sale of goods

**UCC rules:** Between merchants, if within a reasonable time a writing in confirmation of the contract and sufficient against the sender is received, and the party receiving it has reason to know its content, it satisfies the requirement of the Statute of Frauds against such party unless written notice of objection to its contents is given within ten days after it is received.

A contract that does not satisfy the general rule, but which is valid in other respects is enforceable if:

1) the goods are to be specifically manufactured for the buyer and are not suitable for sale to others in the ordinary course of the seller's business, and the seller, before notice of repudiation is received and under circumstances which reasonably indicated that the goods are for the buyer, has made either a substantial beginning of manufacture or commitments for their procurement, or

2) the party against whom enforcement is sought admits in pleadings, testimony, or in court that a contract for sale was made, but the contract is not enforceable under this provision beyond the number of goods admitted, or

3) for goods for which payment has been made or accepted or which have been received or accepted.

If, as modified, a UCC contract involves a sale of goods for more than $500, it requires compliance with the Statute of Frauds.

### Suretyship

An oral promise to pay another's debt is usually unenforceable because of the Statute of Frauds.

If the primary purpose of the promise to pay another's debt is to further the promisor's goals, the promise is enforceable even if there is no memorandum signed by the promisor sufficient to satisfy the Statute of Frauds.

In addition to the writing required by the Statute of Frauds, a party seeking to collect from a surety must give reasonable notice to the surety that they have extended credit to the other party to the contract.

The suretyship provisions of the Statute of Frauds are inapplicable unless there is:

1) a contractual relationship between the creditor and the party who is to benefit from the services, and

2) the creditor knows that the defendant is acting in a suretyship capacity rather than in a direct contractual capacity.

*Notes for active learning*

## Parol Evidence Rule

The *parol evidence* rule bars evidence of prior or contemporaneous statements that contradict the terms of a written contract.

If the written contract is integrated, evidence of prior or contemporaneous agreements between the parties is inadmissible.

### Exceptions to the parol evidence rule

However, *parol evidence* for the terms of a contract is admissible:

1) to prove that there is a condition precedent to a contract's coming into existence;

2) to explain an ambiguity;

3) to show that the parties used words in a nontraditional manner or spoke in code;

4) to prove a mistake in reducing the terms of an oral agreement to writing;

5) to prove contract modification by evidence of conversations after contract formation.

    At common law, a provision in a written agreement that a writing can only modify a contract is not valid;

6) to prove, for an oral contract which is not integrated, subjects not covered by the written contract.

**UCC rules:** The terms to which the confirmatory memoranda of the parties agree, or which are set forth in writing intended by the parties as a final expression of their agreement may not be contradicted by evidence of prior or contemporaneous oral agreement but may be explained or supplemented by:

1) *course of dealing*, *usage of trade*, or *course of performance*, or

2) evidence of consistent additional terms unless the court finds the writing was intended as a complete and exclusive statement of the terms of the agreement.

When inconsistent with usage of trade, a course of dealing trumps usage of trade and controls the interpretation of the contract.

Unlike the rule at common law, under the UCC, a signed agreement that excludes modification or rescission except by a signed writing cannot be modified or rescinded.

Except for between merchants, such a requirement on a form supplied by the merchant must be separately signed by the other party.

Although an attempt at modification or rescission does not satisfy the UCC provisions for the Statute of Frauds or *parol evidence* rule, it can operate as a waiver.

*Notes for active learning*

## Interpretation of Contracts

### Employment-at-will

The primary goal in interpreting a contract is to carry out the intent of the parties.

Permanent employment means employment-at-will.

In an employment-at-will relationship, either party can terminate the agreement at any time without termination being a breach unless the termination violates public policy.

> When parties attach significantly different meanings to the same material term, the meaning that controls is that "attached by one of them if at the time the agreement was made . . . that party did not know of any different meaning attached by the other, and the other knew the meaning attached by the first party." Restatement (Second) of Contracts § 201.

### UCC course of dealing and usage of trade

**UCC rules:** A *course of dealing* is a sequence of previous conduct between the parties to a particular transaction, which is reasonably regarded as establishing a common basis of understanding for interpreting their expressions and other conduct.

A *usage of trade* is a practice or method of dealing with such regularity of observance in a place, vocation, or trade to justify an expectation that it will be observed for the transaction in question.

The existence and scope of such usage are to be proved as facts.

If it is established that such a usage is embodied in a written trade code or similar writing, the interpretation of the writing is for the court.

A course of dealing between parties and usage of trade in the vocation or trade in which they are engaged, or of which they are or should be aware, shall give meaning to, and supplement or qualify, terms of an agreement.

The express terms of an agreement and an applicable *course of dealing* or *usage of trade* shall be construed wherever reasonable as consistent with each other.

When such construction is unreasonable, express terms control both the course of dealing and usage of trade, and the course of dealing controls usage of trade.

*Notes for active learning*

## Conditions

### Express conditions

If the obligation of one party to a contract to perform under that contract is subject to an express condition precedent, the other party seeking to establish a breach must either show compliance with an express condition or that the other party was in bad faith for the condition, thereby excusing compliance with the condition.

A contract condition that performance be satisfactory to the purchaser means that an objective standard will be applied, and performance must be satisfactory to a reasonable person.

If the contract involves personal taste, the performance must be subjectively satisfactory to the purchaser.

Even when the subjective standard is applied, the purchaser must act in good faith.

If one party assumes an obligation and the size of which at the time of contracting is unknown, they are entitled to be paid the consideration promised, even if the obligation is substantially smaller than anticipated.

If a certificate of completion by the architect is a condition of completing a construction contract, the builder cannot collect in full under the contract until that certificate is obtained unless they prove that the architect failed to provide it because of bad faith.

If it is clear that the purpose of the condition was to benefit or protect one of the parties, that party may waive the condition and insist that the other party perform.

### Constructive conditions of exchange

If no order of performance is specified in the contract, each party must perform its obligations under the contract as a condition for demanding performance from the other.

For example, in a sale of goods contract, the buyer must pay for the goods, and the seller must deliver the goods simultaneously. Such mutual conditions precedent is constructive conditions of exchange.

The parties to a contract can make the performance by one party a condition precedent to the performance by the other.

Absent a special provision concerning partial payment in the contract; a party has no right to be paid until they complete the required performance.

If the time for performance is not made of the essence, a party may perform in a reasonable time.

## Divisible contracts

A divisible contract occurs when performance by one party of less than the full contractual obligation gives that party a right to require partial performance of the other party's obligation.

For example, if A is employed by B for one year, B will ordinarily have an obligation to pay A a portion of their yearly salary periodically.

If a contract is divisible, one divisible portion's performance permits the plaintiff to demand performance from the defendant for that separable portion, even if the plaintiff is in breach of another separable portion.

For example, if A, the employee on an annual salary with monthly pay periods, works for one month, they are entitled to be paid for that month's work, even if they do not complete the full year's employment.

Contract law acknowledges the fact that parties sometimes embody obligations that are, in most respects, separable into a single document or agreement.

Rules for damages permit the separable parts to be treated separately.

Though the contract has separable components for damages, it is still a single contract permitting the damages suffered by each side to be litigated in a single lawsuit.

If the contract requires one party to perform a single task (e.g., building a structure), the fact that the contract requires periodic payments does not make it a divisible contract.

## Immaterial breach and substantial performance

Under the common law, the plaintiff can sue for breach of contract and collect contract damages if they have substantially performed the contract, even if there is an immaterial (non-willful) breach.

If the plaintiff has not fully performed the contract, the defendant can successfully assert a counterclaim for damages caused by the plaintiff's failure to perform fully.

**UCC rule:** The UCC does not recognize the doctrine of substantial performance. Instead, it follows the rule of *perfect tender*.

Except for an installment contract, the seller must tender the correct amount of conforming goods at the time specified, or the buyer can reject the goods without liability and sue the seller for damages.

## Installment contracts

**UCC rules:** An installment contract is one where the seller does not have an obligation to deliver all the goods to be sold under the contract at one time.

If a contract is determined to be an installment contract, the rule of perfect tender, which permits the buyer to reject non-conforming goods if all goods are to be delivered at one time, is inapplicable.

The buyer can reject a nonconforming shipment only if it substantially impairs the installment value and cannot be cured.

A failure by the seller to deliver the appropriate quantity of conforming goods on time for one installment of an installment contract is a breach of the total contract only if the nonconformity substantially impairs the entire contract's value.

## UCC rule – implied warranty of merchantability

All merchant sellers give implied warranties of merchantability.

UCC § 2-314(2) defines the implied warranty of merchantability:

1) goods, to be merchantable, must at least pass without objection in the trade under the contract description; and
2) in the case of fungible goods are of a fair average quality within the description; and
3) are fit for the ordinary purpose for which goods are used; and
4) run within the variations permitted by the agreement, or even kind of quality and quantity within each unit and among all units involved; and
5) are adequately contained, packaged, and labeled as the agreement may require; and
6) conform to promises or affirmations made on the container or label, if any.

## UCC rule – warranty of fitness for a particular purpose

Under UCC § 2- 315, a warranty of fitness for a particular purpose arises whenever the seller has reason to know of any particular purpose for which the goods are required. The buyer is relying upon the seller's skill to select suitable goods.

### Constructive condition of cooperation

A condition of cooperation is implied in every contract.

A party who wrongfully hinders the other party's performance breaches the contract.

Each party to a contract has an implied duty to cooperate with the other party in achieving the objects of the contract.

### Obligations of good faith and fair dealing

Each party to a contract has an implied duty to act in good faith.

Acting in bad faith can constitute a breach of contract and give the other party a defense to a suit for breach of contract.

### Suspension or excuse of conditions by waiver

A waiver occurs when a party to a contract affirmatively represents to the other party that it will not act on or enforce a known right.

A waiver is revocable unless the other party relies on the waiver to their detriment, or the waiver is an agreement supported by consideration.

The conduct of a contracting party in failing to insist on full performance for some time can constitute a course of dealings and a waiver of the right to full performance during the remainder of the contract if relied upon by the other party to their detriment.

If the certification of a condition's performance is placed in a third party to benefit one of the contracting parties, that contracting party can waive the certification.

**UCC rule:** A party who had made a waiver affecting an executory portion of the contract may retract the waiver by notification to the other party so that strict performance of terms waived will be required unless the retraction would be unjust due to a material change of position in reliance on the waiver.

## Remedies

### Rescission

When a seller induces a buyer's consent to a contract through a material misrepresentation, the resulting contract is voidable at the election of the buyer.

In some cases, a failure to independently inspect property might constitute a defense to a claim of misrepresentation.

The buyer is entitled to rely on the truth of the seller's material representations and need not conduct independent tests to see whether the seller is lying.

### Buyer's and seller's obligations unless terms are specified

**UCC rule:** The seller must tender conforming goods at their place of business at the specified time, and the buyer has a concurrent obligation to pay the purchase price at that time.

### Cure

**UCC rules:** Where tender or delivery by the seller is rejected because it is non-conforming and the time for performance has not yet expired, the seller may timely notify the buyer of the intention to cure and within the contract time make a conforming delivery.

Where the buyer rejects a non-conforming tender which the seller had reasonable grounds to believe to be acceptable with or without money allowance, the seller may, if they seasonably notify the buyer, have a further reasonable time to substitute a conforming tender.

### Rights of the non-breaching party

**UCC rule**: If a party to a contract has committed a material breach, the non-breaching party is excused from further performance of the contract.

### Demand for assurances

**UCC rule:** A contract for the sale of goods imposes an obligation on each party that the other's expectation of receiving due performance will not be impaired.

When reasonable grounds for insecurity arise concerning either party's performance, the other may in writing demand adequate assurance of performance. Until receiving such assurance, if commercially reasonable, the requesting party may suspend performance for which they have not already received the agreed return.

Acceptance of improper delivery or payment does not prejudice the aggrieved party's right to demand adequate future performance assurance.

After receipt of a justified demand, failure to provide within a reasonable time, not exceeding thirty days, such assurance of due performance is adequate under the case's circumstances and is a repudiation of the contract.

### Anticipatory repudiation

Anticipatory repudiation occurs when a party to the contract gives unequivocal notice to the other party that they will not perform their obligations at the time set for performance.

If the non-repudiating party has not relied on anticipatory repudiation by canceling the contract or materially changing their position, the repudiating party may retract the repudiation, providing they give adequate assurances.

The non-repudiating party has no right to sue for a breach before the time of scheduled performance.

**UCC rule:** When either party repudiates the contract concerning a performance not yet due, the loss of which will substantially impair the value of the contract to the other, the aggrieved party may:

1) for a commercially reasonable time await performance by the repudiating party; or

2) resort to a remedy for breach even though they have notified the repudiating party that they would await the latter's performance and has urged retraction; and,

3) in either case, suspend their performance or proceed following this article's provisions on the seller's right to identify goods to the contract notwithstanding the breach or salvage unfinished goods.

### Risk of loss

**UCC rules:** The risk of loss is initially on the seller.

The risk of loss shifts to the buyer when the seller completes delivery obligation for goods that meet the contract's quantity and quality specifications.

If nothing is said about the place of delivery or the contract specifies that delivery is at the seller's place of business, the risk of loss shifts to the buyer when the seller places conforming goods on a common carrier with instructions shipped to the buyer.

If the contract requires delivery at the buyer's place of business, the risk of loss does not shift to the buyer until conforming goods arrive at the buyer's place of business.

If the goods shipped are non-conforming, the seller retains the risk of loss until accepted.

If the buyer initially accepts the goods and rightfully revokes acceptance, the risk of loss is on the buyer only to the extent that the buyer's insurance covers the goods.

### Rights of *bona fide* purchasers

**UCC rule:** A *bona fide* purchaser of goods from a person in the business of selling those goods takes superior title to the true owner of those goods.

### Seller's remedies in the event of buyer's breach

**UCC rules:** The standard measure of damages for non-acceptance or repudiation by the buyer is the difference between the market price at the time and place for tender and the unpaid contract price, together with incidental damages but less expenses saved in consequence of the buyer's breach.

If the measure of damages provided in the preceding paragraph is inadequate to put the seller in as good a position as performance would have done.

The measure of damages is the profit (including reasonable overhead), which the seller would have made from the buyer's full performance, together with incidental damages provided in this article, due allowances for costs reasonably incurred, and due credit for payments or proceeds of resale.

As a limited alternative remedy, the seller may make the goods available to the buyer and sue for the contract price if the goods cannot be sold in the seller's ordinary course of business.

### Buyer's remedies in the event of seller's breach

**UCC rules:** The buyer may seek damages – the difference between the market price and the contract price.

The buyer may fix damages by purchasing the goods elsewhere and collect the difference between the price they pay and the contract price; this remedy is *cover*.

The buyer may tender the full purchase price and seek an order requiring the seller to deliver the goods if they are unique.

### Measure of damages

Expectancy damages are the standard measure of contract damages, i.e., the amount of money that would put them in the same position as if the breaching party had performed their obligations under the contract.

The amount of a non-breaching party's expectancy damages on a contract where the non-breaching party has not expended money towards their obligated performance is the profit they would have made had the contract been performed.

If the non-breaching party has expended money in the performance of their obligations under the contract, they are entitled to recover those sums plus profit.

If expectancy damages are too speculative and cannot be recovered, the non-breaching party is entitled to reliance damages, the amount expended to perform the contract, whether or not those expenditures benefited the breaching party.

If payments on a contract are due in installments and there is no acceleration clause, the non-breaching party can only sue for the unpaid installments.

If a party voluntarily incurs additional expenses toward the performance of the contract after they know that the other party is in breach, they may not recover those additional expenses.

A non-breaching party has a duty to mitigate damages by taking steps to avoid damages they should have foreseen and could have avoided without undue risk, expense, or humiliation.

For example, if the employer breaches an employment contract, the employee must use reasonable efforts to seek substitute employment during the remainder of the contract period.

If they fail to mitigate, the fair value of what they would have received if they had found other employment is deducted from their expectancy damages.

If incurred to mitigate damage after the breach, reasonable expenses are recoverable as incidental damages, even if expenses are not connected to a successful mitigation attempt.

The victim of a breach is entitled to recover only those damages which could not reasonably have been avoided.

Failure to take reasonable steps to mitigate damages defeats a claim for consequential damages.

## Consequential damages

Consequential damages are limited to those damages that were reasonably foreseeable by the parties when the contract is made.

## Liquidated damages

A provision fixing liquidated damages is unenforceable unless the amount fixed is reasonable compared to the damages that the parties could anticipate when making the contract or the damages incurred.

## Specific performance

The buyer and seller are entitled to sue for specific performance of enforceable land contracts.

Specific performance requiring the defendant to perform is not available to remedy a personal services contract.

A negative injunction can be granted by the standards for granting injunctions, preventing the defendant from working for a person other than the one to whom contractually bound.

## Restitution damages (*quantum meruit*)

If a party is prevented from suing on the contract because the contract is unenforceable (e.g., Statute of Frauds) or because they committed a material breach, they are limited to restitution damages.

Restitution (or *quantum meruit*) damages are the fair value of the benefit conferred on the other party.

An unjust enrichment claim cannot exceed the contract price when all the work giving rise to the claim has been performed, and the only remaining obligation is the payment of the price.

Restitution damages cannot be greater than the recoverable damages if the contract were enforceable.

*Notes for active learning*

## Monetary Damages for Breach of Contract Parties

Monetary damages are of three types: compensatory, consequential, and liquidated.

Compensatory damages are intended to compensate a non-breaching party for the loss of the bargain. They place the non-breaching party in the same position as if the contract has been entirely performed by restoring the "benefit of the bargain." Additionally, a non-breaching party can sometimes recover consequential or special damages from the breaching party.

Consequential damages are foreseeable damages that arise from circumstances outside the contract. To be liable for consequential damages, the breaching party must know or have reason to know that the breach will cause special damages to the other party.

Moreover, under certain circumstances, the parties to a contract may agree in advance to the amount of damages payable upon a breach of contract as *liquidated damages*. To be lawful, the damages must be difficult or impracticable to determine, and the liquidated amount must be reasonable in the circumstances. An enforceable liquidated damage clause is an exclusive remedy even if actual damages are later determined to be different.

A liquidated damages clause is considered a penalty if actual damages are determinable in advance or the liquidated damages are excessive or unconscionable, in which case the liquidated damages clause is unenforceable. The non-breaching party may then seek actual damages.

*Notes for active learning*

## Impossibility and Frustration

### Impossibility of performance

If events after the formation of a contract make the performance by one party illegal or impossible, the doctrine of impossibility is applicable, and the parties are discharged from their contractual obligations.

The doctrine of impossibility applies at common law when the contract's subject matter is destroyed, or a party to a personal service contract dies.

The destruction of an existing structure renders a contract to repair it impossible, terminating the contract.

The contractor has the right to collect for the fair value of the work done in *quantum meruit* but cannot sue for contract damages because the contract obligations have been discharged.

A party may not rely on the defense of impossibility if they expressly assume the risk of performing an objectively impossible obligation.

### Excused performance under the UCC

**UCC rules:** Under the doctrine of impracticability, performance is excused when:

1) goods identified to the contract are destroyed,

2) performance becomes illegal,

3) performance is prevented by a non-foreseeable event, the nonoccurrence of a basic assumption of the contract.

Under § 2-615, when a contract specifies produce to be grown on a specific farm and the crop is destroyed by natural forces beyond the farmer's control, the farmer is excused from performance to the extent of the damage.

*Notes for active learning*

## Conflict of Laws in Contracts

### Place of contracting

Contracts – *lex loci contractus* ("*law of the place where the contract is made*") applies.

Issues concerning performance are governed by the law of the place of performance.

The forum decides where the contract was made.

The state whose law is applied to the dispute may have no interests at stake (other than being the place of contracting).

Where the contract is made is subject to interpretation based upon the nature of the modern commercial transaction.

The issue may be characterized as one of performance to apply different laws and achieve the desired result. In *Louis-Dreyfus v. Paterson Steamships, Ltd* (1930), each state favored limiting liability, but the *lex loci* rule did not. To advance the interests of the involved states, the court characterized the dispute as performance.

Contracts – party expectations may determine the choice of law.

A court may ignore the *lex loci* law and apply the law of the place of performance to resolve a contract dispute if it determines that the parties entered into their obligation because of that law (contract is invalid under *lex loci* law but enforceable in place of performance)

An adhesion contract (steamship ticket) may designate the law to be applied regardless of *lex loci* if the forum selected has some connection to the agreement.

Usury – courts tend to apply whichever law upholds the validity of the contract if there is a reasonable relationship to the transaction and the parties were in equal bargaining positions.

$2^{nd}$ Restatement § 203 usury – a contract is enforceable if its interest rate is permitted in a state with a substantial relationship to the contract and does not significantly exceed the price allowed by an interested state.

The presumption of validity is necessary to promote the free flow of commerce; otherwise, lenders may be reluctant to lend money.

Rights under a contract vest at the moment the contract is made.

Clear rules but may lead to a state with no policy interest in the outcome of the litigation.

American rule: the place of contract for specific issues (e.g., validity, capacity).

The place of contract determines capacity.

## Special rules

Special rules determine where the contract is made depending on the type of conflict.

§311 Place of contracting: principal event necessary to make a contract occurs.

§312 Formal contract: effective on delivery, place of contracting is where delivery is made.

§323 Informal unilateral contract: where the event takes place that makes it binding.

§325 Informal bilateral contract: where the second promise is made in consideration of the first promise.

§326 Acceptance from one state to another: if acceptance is sent by an agent of the acceptor, the state where the agent delivers it or from which acceptance is sent.

§332 Validity and effect of the contract: the law of the place where the contract was made (capacity, necessary form, consideration, requirements to make a promise binding, time, and place where the promise is to be performed, the character of the promise).

§358: performance handled with the place where a contract is to be performed (i.e., manner, time, locality, parties involved, sufficiency, an excuse for non-performance).

Justifiable expectations of parties are enforceable.

## Place of performance for other issues

Old law: the law only if there is a connection.

If a contract is completed in another state, it makes no difference whether the person goes in person, sends an agent, or writes a letter across the boundary lines between the states.

English rule: parties' intent, if unclear, is the "closest and most real connection."

Rome Convention eliminated "mandatory rules," replacing them with "overriding mandatory provisions."

Party autonomy – parties may choose but be limited by "mandatory rules" of the country where the contract was made.

A court can apply its law if it considers the law "overriding," providing much discretion.

Default rule (absent choice) § 4 – "most closely connected."

Presumption (closest connection) § 4(2) – "characteristic performance."

A contract's validity is to be decided by the law of the place where the contract is made unless it is to be performed in another country.

If the contract is to be performed in another place as intended by the parties, the validity, nature, obligation, and interpretation are governed by the location of performance.

Freedom of contract dominates in most states, with some restrictions (2$^{nd}$ Restatement).

Juenger – parties should be free to select their own rules that reflect commercial practice and the best law without regard for the desires of sovereigns.

## Applying choice-of-law rules to specific issues

For contracts, the difficulties and complexities involved have prevented the courts from formulating precise rules, which provide satisfactory accommodation of the underlying factors in situations that may arise.

Courts state the general principle, such as applying the local law "of the state of the most significant relationship," to provide perspective about the correct approach but this approach does not furnish precise answers.

The courts must look at the underlying factors to arrive at a decision.

A statement of precise rules in choice of law is complicated by the variety of facts and issues.

Many of these issues have not been thoroughly explored by the courts. These rules represent general statements frequently used by the courts in opinions and the rationale of the decisions in more recent opinions.

*Notes for active learning*

## Establishing Agency

Agency relationships are generally formed by the mutual consent of a principal and an agent, although not always. An agency can arise as an express agency, implied agency, apparent agency, and agency by ratification. The most common form of agency is express agency. In an express agency, the agent has the authority to contract or otherwise act on the principal's behalf as expressly stated in the agency agreement. Additionally, the agent may possess certain implied or apparent authority to act on the principal's behalf.

*Express agency* occurs when a principal and an agent expressly agree to enter into an agency agreement with each other. Express agency contracts can be oral or written unless the Statute of Frauds stipulates that they must be written. A power of attorney is an example of an express agency. An implied agency is an agency that occurs from the parties' conduct rather than from a prior agreement between them. The facts determine the extent of the agent's authority.

*Implied authority* can be conferred by *industry custom*, *prior dealing between the parties*, the agent's position, and acts deemed necessary to carry out the agent's duties.

*Apparent agency* (or *agency by estoppel*) arises when a principal creates the appearance of an agency that does not exist. Where an apparent agency is established, the principal is estopped from denying the agency relationship and is bound to contracts entered into by the apparent agent while acting within the scope of the apparent agency. The principal's actions (not the agent's) create an apparent agency.

An *agency by ratification* occurs when a person misrepresents themselves as another's agent when they are not, and the purported principal ratifies (accepts) the unauthorized act. In such cases, the principal is bound to perform, and the agent is relieved of liability for misrepresentation.

*Notes for active learning*

*Governing Law*

## Contract Law – Quick Facts

1. A **gratuitous assignee** has rights under a contract that *may* be enforced against the **obligor** *until or unless* the assignment is revoked.

2. Where there is a **delegation of duties**, the delegator *and* the delegate are *liable* for the performance of the agreement.

3. Under UCC, a **crop failure** resulting from an unexpected cause excuses a farmer's obligation to deliver the full amount if they make a fair and reasonable allocation among their buyers, which could be allocated *pro-rata* between buyers.

   The buyer may accept the proposed modification *or* terminate the contract.

4. The general rule is that a **contractor** is responsible for destroying the premises under construction *prior to completion*; once the residence is complete, the **risk of loss** shifts to the owner.

5. **Performance is excused** where it is prevented by the **operation of law**, despite stipulations to the contrary; governmental interference makes the contract's performance illegal. The party may be excused from the performance.

6. A **detriment** exists whenever a promisee gives up the **legal right** to do something, regardless of whether they would have done otherwise.

7. Under UCC, a **written confirmation** is sufficient as an acceptance even though it states additional terms *unless* the acceptance is **expressly made conditional on assent** to the additional terms.

8. An **implied-in-fact** contract is formed by *mutual manifestations of assent* (i.e., conduct) other than oral or written language. Even if there is no mutual assent, the parties are bound if their conduct objectively manifests contractual intent.

9. **Assignment and delegation** are prohibited where they would substantially alter the obligor's risks, such as an **exoneration clause**, which effectively holds the obligor accountable (liable) for the obligee's actions.

10. A **novation** substitutes a new party for an original party to the contract—requires the assent of *all* parties and completely releases the original party.

11. **Despite reliance**, a third-party **donee beneficiary** has *no* cause of action against the promise because the promisor's act is gratuitous. The promisor may *not* be held to it *unless* they have directly created the reliance by personally informing the beneficiary.

12. Where there is an **oral condition precedent**, evidence of the condition falls outside the *parol evidence rule*.

*Notes for active learning*

## Relationship matrix

*Notes for active learning*

## Review Questions

**Multiple-choice questions**

1. Examples of enforceable agreements are:

    I. Sales contracts
    II. Rental agreements
    III. Licensing agreements

    **A.** I only
    **B.** I and II only
    **C.** II and III only
    **D.** I, II and III

2. Article 2 of the UCC applies to merchants for:

    **A.** Sales of at least $100
    **B.** Sales of goods
    **C.** Sales of services
    **D.** Commercial leases

3. Contracts made by minors are:

    **A.** Void
    **B.** Voidable
    **C.** Executory
    **D.** Executed

4. An *agreement* involves:

    I. An offer
    II. An offeree
    III. An offerer

    **A.** I only
    **B.** I and II only
    **C.** I and III only
    **D.** I, II and III

5. If the potential groom backs out late in an engagement, he may:

    I. Be sued under a breach of contract theory
    II. Counter-sue if he feels he was not to blame
    III. Be responsible for items contracted for the marriage ceremony

    **A.** I only
    **B.** I and II only
    **C.** I and III only
    **D.** III only

**6.** In a contract, the offeree:

**A.** makes an offer
**B.** tenders an offer
**C.** promises to do something
**D.** has the power to create a contract

**7.** A counteroffer:

  I. Terminates the offeror's offer
  II. Creates a new offer
  III. Binds the recipient

**A.** I only
**B.** I and II only
**C.** II only
**D.** I, II and III

**8.** The following is NOT a requirement of an effective offer:

**A.** The offer must be accepted according to the mirror-image rule
**B.** The offer must be seriously intended
**C.** The terms must be definite or reasonably certain
**D.** The offer must be made to the offeree

**9.** In the evolution of contracts, the following is NOT true:

**A.** The use of contracts goes back to ancient times
**B.** The common law of contracts developed in France around the 18th century
**C.** The United States adopted a *laissez-faire* approach to contracts
**D.** None of the above

**10.** Contracts to engage in illegal activity are.

**A.** Void
**B.** Voidable
**C.** Executory
**D.** Executed

**11.** Under common law, an offeror may *revoke an offer*:

**A.** At any time
**B.** After the offeree has rejected the offer
**C.** After the offeree accepts the offer
**D.** Before the acceptance of the offer

**12.** The following are requirements for an enforceable contract, EXCEPT:

**A.** Consideration
**B.** Contractual capacity
**C.** Agreement
**D.** Counteroffer

**13.** *Consideration* may involve:

  I. Money
  II. Performance of an act
  III. Property

**A.** I only
**B.** II only
**C.** I and III only
**D.** I, II and III

**14.** According to the statute of frauds, contracts that are not in writing, but should be, are:

**A.** Void
**B.** Enforceable
**C.** Unenforceable
**D.** Illegal

**15.** The following is an example of an equitable remedy:

**A.** Liquidated damages
**B.** Punitive damages
**C.** Tender of performance
**D.** Specific performance

**16.** A nondisclosure agreement does NOT:

**A.** Provide for the equitable sharing of information
**B.** Swear the signatory to secrecy
**C.** Usually involve takeovers and corporate deals
**D.** Protect people that have great ideas

**17.** A contract to perform an illegal act is:

  I. An enforceable private agreement
  II. Void
  III. Unenforceable

**A.** I only
**B.** II only
**C.** III only
**D.** II and III only

**18.** The following have the burden of proof of the incapacity to contract:

  I. The minor
  II. The guardian
  III. The conservator

**A.** I only
**B.** I and II only
**C.** III only
**D.** I, II and III

*Law Essentials: Contracts*

## True/false questions

**19.** An offeror must objectively intend to be bound by the offer.

　　　True　　　　　False

**20.** Contracts are involuntary agreements entered into by parties.

　　　True　　　　　False

**21.** A contract may be made by implication of the parties' conduct.

　　　True　　　　　False

**22.** An offer does not need to be communicated to the offeree.

　　　True　　　　　False

**23.** A contract is an agreement that is enforceable in a court of law.

　　　True　　　　　False

**24.** In an option contract, the offeror cannot sell to another during the option period.

　　　True　　　　　False

**25.** The object of the contract may be for any purpose.

　　　True　　　　　False

**26.** "Are you interested in selling your boat for $8,200?" is an offer.

　　　True　　　　　False

**27.** Special rules have been developed for electronic commerce.

　　　True　　　　　False

**28.** A counteroffer is a rejection.

　　　True　　　　　False

**29.** An offeror may revoke an offer before acceptance after it has been made to the offeree.

　　　True　　　　　False

**30.** The party making the offer is the offeree.

　　　True　　　　　False

**31.** The terms of a contract become private law between the parties.

　　　True　　　　　False

**32.** Contracts entered into by minors are void.

　　　True　　　　　False

**33.** To have an enforceable contract, there must be an agreement between the parties.

　　　True　　　　　False

**34.** The UCC, Article 2 governs the sale of goods by nonmerchants.

　　　True　　　　　False

**35.** If a bride-to-be breaks the engagement, they must return the engagement ring.

　　　True　　　　　False

**36.** Intended third-party beneficiaries have contract rights.

　　　True　　　　　False

**Answer keys**

1: D  11: D
2: B  12: D
3: B  13: D
4: D  14: C
5: D  15: D
6: D  16: A
7: B  17: D
8: A  18: D
9: B
10: A

19: True  31: True
20: False  32: False
21: True  33: True
22: False  34: False
23: True  35: True
24: True  36: True
25: False
26: False
27: True
28: True
29: True
30: False

# Bar Exam Information, Preparation
## and
## Test-Taking Strategies

**STERLING**
Test Prep

## Introduction to the Uniform Bar Examination (UBE)

### Structure of the UBE

The Uniform Bar Examination (UBE) includes 1) the Multistate Bar Examination (MBE), 2) Multistate Essay Examination (MEE), and 3) Multistate Performance Test (MPT).

The MBE has 200 multiple-choice questions accounting for 50% of the UBE.

The MEE has six essays worth 30% of the UBE score.

The MPT has two legal tasks (e.g., complaint, client letter) for 20% of the UBE score.

### The Multistate Bar Examination (MBE)

The Multistate Bar Examination consists of 200 four-option multiple-choice questions prepared by the National Conference of Bar Examiners (NCBE).

Of these 200 questions, 175 are scored, and 25 are unscored pretest questions.

Candidates answer 100 questions in the three-hour morning session and the remaining 100 questions in the three-hour afternoon session.

The 175 scored questions are distributed with 25 questions on each of the seven subject areas: Federal Civil Procedure, Constitutional Law, Contracts, Criminal Law and Procedure, Evidence, Real Property, and Torts.

A specified percentage of questions in each subject tests topics in those subjects.

For example, approximately one-third of Evidence questions test hearsay and its exceptions, while approximately one-third of Torts questions test negligence.

### Interpreting the UBE score report

**Overall score.** The National Conference of Bar Examiners (NCBE) states the Uniform Bar Exam (UBE) requires a passing scaled score between 260 to 280. Scores above 280 receive a passing score in every UBE state.

The "percentile" is the number of people that scored lower. If an examinee scored in the 47th percentile, they scored higher than 47% of the examinees (and lower than 53%).

The examinee is first given a "raw score,"; based on the number of correct answers.

The raw score is adjusted by adding points to achieve the "scaled score." The number of points added is determined by a formula that compares the difficulty of the current exam to prior benchmark exams.

The comparative performance of examinees on "control questions" (prior pretest questions) given on previous exams form the basis for determining each exam's difficulty.

**MBE scaled score.** Examinees receive a scaled score and not an MBE "raw" score (i.e., the number of correct answers). MBE scores are scaled scores calculated by the NCBE through a statistical process used for standardized tests.

According to the NCBE, this statistical process adjusts raw scores on the current exam to account for differences in difficulty compared to previously administered exams. The scaled score is calculated from the raw score, but the NCBE does not publish the conversion formula.

Since the MBE is a scaled score, equating makes it impossible to know precisely how many questions must be answered correctly to receive a particular score. Equating allows scores from different exams to be compared since a specific scaled score represents the same level of knowledge among exams.

The MBE is curved, so just because a score is "close" to passing does not mean you are close. For example, a 124 may be in the 31st percentile and a 136 in the 62nd percentile. A 12-point difference in scaled scores equates to a 31-point percentile difference. If you are in the 120s, much preparation is needed to increase your score.

For most states, aim for a scaled score of 135 to "pass" the MBE. If you are unsure what score you need, divide the passing score by two. For example, if a 270 is needed to pass the bar, divide 268 by two to yield 135 as a threshold score on the MBE.

### The importance of the MBE score

A passing MBE score depends on the jurisdiction. In jurisdictions that score on a 200-point scale, the passing score is the overall score. Passing scores are often approximately 135.

For the July 2020 bar exam, the national average MBE score was 146.1, an increase of 5 points from the July 2019 national average of 141.1.

For comparison, on the July 2018 bar, the national average MBE score was 139.5, a decrease of about 2.2 points from the July 2017 national average of 141.7.

How much the MBE contributes depends on the jurisdiction. Each jurisdiction has its policy for the relative weight given to the MBE compared to other bar exam components.

For Uniform Bar Examination (UBE) jurisdictions, the MBE component is 50%.

Most jurisdictions combine the MBE score with the state essay exam score.

The overall state candidates' performance on the MBE controls the raw state essay's conversion to scaled scores. Achieve a scaled MBE score of at least 135 to pass the bar.

## MEE and MPT scores

In a UBE score report, there are six scores for the Multistate Essay Exam (MEE) and two for the Multistate Performance Test (MPT). Most states release this information.

Most states grade on a 1–6 scale (some use another scale).

In states grading on a 1–6 scale, 4 is considered a passing score.

The MEE and MPT sections are not weighted equally.

The MEE essays are worth 60%, while the MPT is 40% of the written score.

Many examinees assume that they passed the MPT and MEE portions of the exam. Examine the score report to see how you performed on these portions.

## The objective of the Multistate Bar Exam

Working knowledge of the MBE objectives, the skills it tests, how it is drafted, the relationship of the parts of an MBE question, and the testing limitations provide you a substantial advantage in choosing the correct answers to MBE questions and passing the bar.

Knowing which issues are tested and the form in which they are tested makes it more manageable to learn the large body of substantive law.

The MBE's fundamental objective is to measure fairly, and efficiently which law school graduates have the necessary academic qualifications to be admitted to the bar and exceed this threshold.

The multiple-choice exam used to accomplish this objective must be of a consistent level of difficulty.

The level at which the pass decision is made must be achievable by most candidates.

The MBE tests the following skills:

- reading carefully and critically
- identifying the legal issue in a set of facts
- knowing the law that governs the legal issues tested
- distinguish between frequently confused closely-related principles
- making reasonable judgments from ambiguous facts
- understanding how limiting words make plausible-sounding choices wrong
- choosing the correct answer by intelligently eliminating incorrect choices

*Notes for active learning*

## Preparation Strategies for the Bar Exam

### An effective bar exam study plan

There are a lot of great ideas about how to prepare. Follow through with these ideas and turn them into persistent action for successful preparation.

A detailed and well-planned study schedule has benefits, such as giving you a sense of control and building confidence and proficiency.

Pick a date about 12-14 weeks before the exam (November for the February exam and April for the July exam) and use it as the start of your active study period.

Start a month earlier than many others to have a month to review as final preparation at the end.

Students have found this effective. Use an elongated prep period as a study schedule.

Most examinees prefer at least two weeks before the exam to review the material.

By planning early, you will have more time. You may want three or four final weeks to review subjects, take timed exams, and ensure that you are prepared to take the exam.

A few notes on schedule management:

> Do not *start* memorizing during your initial review period. You should be learning every week from the beginning of your study schedule. This final prep period is for reviewing and taking timed exams.
>
> If you stretch the study schedule over several months, plan review weeks into your schedule. For example, every four weeks, use a few days to review the governing law and take timed exams. This is a practical and fruitful approach as you will be more likely to retain the information.

Pick specific dates for specific tasks; this makes it more likely you will complete them.

Make sure the tasks are measurable. (e.g., practice two MEE essays).

Be realistic about the tasks, time, energy, and your ability to complete the items listed as tasks in preparation for the exam.

Remember to take some scheduled breaks from studying.

Exercise, sleep and take care of your physical and mental health.

If you are not in the right mental state preparing for the exam, you will likely be ineffective when studying and are less likely to pass the exam.

## Focused studying

Some people are better at multiple-choice questions; others do better with essays.

The multiple-choice portion (MBE at 50%) and the essay portion (MEE at 30% and MPT at 20%) are weighted equally.

Doing poorly in one section means it will be challenging to achieve a passing score.

Identify weaknesses early in the preparation process and focus on them.

If you struggle with multiple-choice questions, dedicate extra time to practicing MBE questions.

If you struggle with writing, focus on completing MEE essays and complete MPT practice materials.

By reviewing your performance on released multiple-choice practice tests, be concerned if you consistently miss questions that are most answered correctly.

If you have problems with questions and perform below 50%, you lack the fundamental knowledge necessary to pass the MBE.

When reviewing your answers to practice questions, it is essential to review all questions and answers, even those you got right.

Make sure you got that correct answer for the right reason.

Reviewing the questions and answers is critical for success on the exam.

Spend time reviewing those basic principles and working deliberately on the straightforward (and easy) questions that supplement learning.

## Advice on using outlines

As a user of this governing law book, several of the following points are moot. They are included, so you can be confident that you are using the proper resources to prep for the bar.

Having a useful governing law study guide (such as this book) is critical.

Without effective resources, it is challenging to understand, learn and apply the governing law to the facts given in the question.

Some students use outlines that make learning difficult.

A few common mistakes about outlines:

- Learning outlines that are too long (e.g., more than 100 pages per subject) or too short (e.g., a seven-page Contracts outline). You will be overwhelmed by information or never learn enough governing law.

- Spending too much time comparing several outlines for the same subject.

  For example, using different Contracts outlines and needlessly comparing them. This confusion results in an undue focus on insignificant discrepancies.

- Outlining every subject. If you are not starting to study early, this consumes too much study time. Do not attempt to outline all subjects. It may be a good idea to outline a select few problematic subjects.

Using a detailed and well-organized governing law outline (e.g., this book) is essential; it saves time, organizes concepts, reduces anxiety, and helps you score well and pass the bar.

### Easy questions make the difference

Limitations on the examiners lead to the first important insight into preparation for the exam – the kind of questions that decide whether you pass.

Performance on specific questions correlates with success or failure on the bar.

By analyzing statistics, questions predicting success or failure have been identified.

In general, the most challenging questions were not particularly good predictors of failure because most people who missed them passed the bar.

However, many of the straightforward questions were excellent predictors of success.

The median raw score ranges from about 60% to 66% correct on the MBE.

The National Conference of Bar Examiners (NCBE) writes, "expert panelists reported that they believed MBE items were generally easy, correctly estimating that about 66% of candidates would select the right answer to a typical item."

Depending on the exam's difficulty, in most states, scoring slightly below the median (miss up to 80 questions) still passes.

The most important questions to determine if you pass are not the exceedingly challenging ones but the easy ones where 90% of the examinees answer correctly.

The easy questions usually test a basic and regularly tested point of substantive law.

The wrong choices (i.e., the distracters) are typically easy to eliminate.

Your first task in preparing for the MBE is to get easy questions correct.

## Study plan based upon statistics

These statistics show that an excellent performance on either the MBE questions (approximately 67% correct) or the state essays (4s on essays) assures you a passing score.

If you fail the MBE by 9 points or the essays by 5 points, the probability of passing the bar is in the single digits.

Put effort into performing well on the MBE questions for the following reasons.

- The questions are objective, and there are enough questions that are predictable concerning content and structure that it is possible, through reasonable effort, to answer 67% of the questions correctly.

- Studying the MBE first has the added advantage of preparing the necessary substantive law for state essays.

- The essays cover several subjects, the precise topic tested is unpredictable, and the answers are graded subjectively by graders who work quickly.

You had three years of law school practice with essays and less experience with multiple-choice questions.

Master the MBE before spending time preparing for the essays.

## Factors associated with passing the bar

Based on an analysis of statistics from students' performance, the following factors predict the likelihood of passing the bar:

LSAT score

First-year Grade Point Average (GPA)

LSAT scores are a significant predictor of success on the bar because the LSAT requires similar multiple-choice test-taking skills as the MBE.

The LSAT tests many of the types of legal reasoning tested on the MBE.

A lower LSAT can be overcome by a comprehensive study of the MBE governing law, but these students must work harder.

Most of the subjects tested (e.g., constitutional law, civil procedure, contracts, criminal law, real property, torts) on the MBE are taken in the first year of law school.

First-year GPA measures mastery of subjects, preparedness for exams, and the ability to understand legal principles and apply them to given fact patterns.

The MBE measures the same factors but in a multiple-choice format instead of essays.

### Pass rates based on GPA and LSAT scores

Past statistics indicate that law students with LSAT scores above 155 and a first-year GPA above 3.0 are reasonably assured of passing the bar.

They should study conscientiously and take practice MBEs to perform at the level needed, but they have little cause to panic.

Students with LSAT scores between 150 and 155 and a first-year GPA between 2.5 and 3.0 are in a bit more danger of failing and need to undertake rigorous preparation.

They must achieve a scaled score of 135 and take released practice exams and understand the reasons for incorrect choices. They should prepare for state essays by learning the governing laws in this book.

Students with LSAT scores between 145 and 150 and a first-year GPA between 2.2 and 2.5 have a moderate chance of passing the bar from deliberate efforts.

These students should not rely on ordinary commercial bar reviews and need intense training, particularly on the MBE component of the bar. They must devote 50-60 hours per week for seven weeks to prepare for the bar by learning the format and content of substantive law tested on the MBE. They should take released practice exams under exam conditions and conscientiously study the questions missed.

Students with LSAT scores below 145 and a GPA below 2.2 have had a failure rate of approximately 80%.

They must prep faithfully and conscientiously beyond the advice above and must engage in a rigorous course of study, more than is demanded by a traditional bar review course.

*Notes for active learning*

## Learning and Applying the Substantive Law

**Knowledge of substantive law**

The fundamental reason for missing a question is 1) a failure to know the principle of law controlling the answer or 2) failure to understand how that principle is applied.

You must know and apply the governing law to pass the bar. If you do not know the governing law, you will not apply it to answer correctly.

Many students *think* they understand the governing law but do not know the nuances. Do not assume that you understand the governing (i.e., substantive) law. It is prevalent for students not to know the governing law well.

Re-learn the substantive and procedural law taught in first-year courses.

A major mistake is not to memorize the governing law outlined in this book.

The multiple-choice and essay portions test nuances and details of governing law. It is essential to analyze the governing law as it is applied in the context of the question.

On the multiple-choice section, many questions require fine-line distinctions between similar principles of law.

Several multiple-choice answers will *seem* correct, given the limited time to answer. If your knowledge of the governing law is suboptimal, you will not make these subtle distinctions and will have to guess on many questions.

For the essay to be developed, you must know the governing law and apply it to the issues within the call of the question.

If you do not know the governing law, you will not state the correct rule in your essay. You will be unable to apply the correct rule to the fact pattern.

## Where to find the law

The questions must be related to the subject matter outlined in the bar examiners' (NCBE) materials.

While the NCBE outline is broad and ambiguous, years of experience with the exam delineate the scope of material you must learn.

The governing law covered in this book is foundational to the exam. The governing law statements were compiled by analyzing questions released by the multistate examiners. The analysis revealed a limited number of legal principles repeatedly tested.

Review these principles before taking practice exams and understand how they are applied to obtain the correct answer.

The property questions are probably the most difficult. The fact patterns are usually long and involve many parties in complex transactions.

In preparing for the exam, learn basic property principles and apply them. However, extensive studying into property law's crevices is not necessary to score well on these questions.

Feel confident that you do not have to go beyond the information provided in this book to find the governing law.

## Controlling authority

The examiners have specified the sources of authority for the correct answers.

In Constitutional Law and Criminal Procedure, it is Supreme Court decisions.

In Criminal Law, it is common law.

In Evidence, the Federal Rules of Evidence controls.

In Torts and Property, it is the generally accepted view of United States law.

The UCC is the controlling authority in sales (Article 2) questions.

The NCBE released questions, and the published answers determine the controlling law through deduction.

### Recent changes in the law

The exam is prepared months before it is given because of logistical requirements. Therefore, the examiners cannot incorporate recent changes in the law into the questions.

Recent changes in the law will not form the basis for correct answers.

If a recent change makes an answer initially designated as the correct answer to be incorrect, the examiners will credit more than one answer.

The recent holding of a Supreme Court case will not be tested for about two years since the decision was published.

### Lesser-known issues and unusual applications

Some of the challenging exam questions are based on obscure principles of law.

Missing the most challenging questions will not cause you to fail the exam if you have a solid understanding of the governing law. You can learn these principles and answer the question correctly, thereby improving your overall performance.

There are instances where the correct answers are different from the usual rules.

For example, hearsay evidence inadmissible at trial is admissible before a judge hearing evidence on a preliminary question of fact (e.g., Federal Rules of Evidence 104(a)).

### Practice applying the governing law

Some students know the governing law but have problems *applying* it to the facts.

The exam is as much about testing skills as it is about testing the governing law.

Therefore, knowledge of the governing law is not enough to pass.

You must practice answering multiple-choice questions and writing well-organized, coherent, and complete essays where you apply the governing law to the given facts.

*Law Essentials: Contracts*

### Know which governing law is being tested

A typical wrong answer (i.e., distracter) on a question is an answer which is correct under a body of law other than the governing law being tested.

An example is a question governed by Article 2 of the Uniform Commercial Code (UCC), where an offer is irrevocable if:

1) it is in writing,

2) made by a merchant, and

3) states that it is irrevocable.

One of the wrong answers states the correct rule under the common law of contracts, where an offer is revocable unless consideration is paid (i.e., an option) for the promise to keep it open.

### Answers which are always wrong

Some commonly used distracters are always wrong and can be eliminated quickly.

For example, a choice in an evidence question says, "character can only be attacked by reputation evidence." This choice is wrong because both opinion and reputation evidence is admissible under the Federal Rules of Evidence when character attacks are permissible.

## Honing Reading Skills

Reading skills are critical. The basic level is reading to understand the facts, identify the issue and keep the parties distinct. A mistake at this juncture results in answering incorrectly, no matter how much law is known.

### Understanding complex transactions

If the question involves a transaction with many parties, diagram the transaction before analyzing the choices.

The diagram should show the relationship between the parties (e.g., grantor-grantee, assignor-assignee), the transaction date, and the person's relationships in the transaction (e.g., donee, *bona fide* purchaser).

### Impediments to careful reading

Two reasons candidates fail to read carefully are:

1) hurrying through a question,

2) fatigue due to a lack of sleep or strain caused by the exam.

A careful test taker maintains a steady, deliberate pace during the exam. Practice in advance and be well-rested on the test day.

### Reading too much into a question

The examiners are committed to designing questions, which are "a fair index of whether the applicant has the ability to practice law." Psychometric experts ensure that they are fair and unbiased.

Even though you must read every word of these carefully drafted questions, do not read the question to find some bizarre interpretation.

The examiners must ask fair questions and not rely on "tricks." Reading too much into a question and looking for a trick lurking behind every fact leads to the wrong answer often.

It is the straightforward questions that determine whether you pass, not the occasional challenging question that tests some arcane principle of law.

Therefore, take questions at face value.

### Read the call of the question first

Before reading the facts, read the call of the question because it indicates the task for selecting the correct answer. This perspective focuses your attention before reading the facts.

The question contains many *words of art*, such as "most likely," "best defense," or "least likely," which govern the correct answer.

The call is often phrased positively; the "best argument" or "most likely result."

Read answers for consistency with the question and eliminate inconsistent choices.

### Negative calls

When the call of the question is negative, asking for the "weakest argument" or asking which of the options is "not" in a specified category, examine each option with the perspective that the choice with those negative characteristics is the correct answer.

After reading and understanding the question stem, read the call of the question again before reading the choices.

Analyze each choice with the requirements specified in the call of the question.

### Read all choices

Never pick an answer until carefully reading all the choices. The objective is to pick the best answer, which cannot be determined until comparing the choices.

Sometimes the difference between the right and wrong answer is that one choice is more detailed or precisely sets forth the applicable law. You do not know that until reading all the answers carefully.

### Broad statements of black letter law may be correct

When reading an answer, do not rule out choices with imprecise statements of the applicable *black letter* law.

If the examiners always included a choice that was precisely on point, the questions would be too easy. Instead, they often disguise the wording used in the correct answer.

For example, the Federal Rules of Evidence contain an elaborate set of relevancy rules that limit the right to introduce evidence of repairs after an accident. If there was a question where the introduction of that evidence was permissible, and no choices specifically cite the exception to the general rule of exclusion, an answer phrased with the general rule of relevancy "Admissible because its probative value outweighs its prejudicial effect," would be the correct answer.

## Multiple-Choice Test-Taking Tactics

**Determine the single correct answer**

Increase the odds of picking the correct answer based on technical factors independent of substantive (governing) law knowledge.

The examiners' limitation is that every question must have one demonstrably correct and three demonstrably incorrect answers, limiting how the examiners write the choices.

From the question's construction, this limitation may give clues about the answer.

**Process of elimination**

Answering a multiple-choice question is not finding the ideal answer to the question asked but instead picking the best option.

Eliminate choices and evaluate the remaining choice for plausibility.

Eliminate choices that state an incorrect proposition of law or do not relate to the facts.

If you eliminate three options and the remaining one is acceptable, pick it and move on.

**Elimination increases the odds**

It takes about 125 correct answers to pass the MBE. An important strategy in reaching that number is intelligently eliminating choices.

If you are sure of the answer to only 50 of the 200 questions on the exam and confidently eliminate two of the four choices on the remaining 150 questions. Guess between the two remaining choices, and the odds predict 75 correct.

Those 75 correct, coupled with 50 questions you were confident of the answer, produce a raw score of 125 on the MBE and a scaled score above the benchmark 135.

Unfortunately, you cannot avoid guessing on questions, but intelligent methods reduce options to only two viable choices.

Sometimes you might not be able to eliminate the wrong answers just because you are sure of the answer to one of the choices. Eliminating with confidence even one choice increases the probability of correctly answering the question.

Law Essentials: Contracts

### Eliminating two wrong answers

Specific questions on the MBE are challenging because of distinguishing between two choices when selecting the best answer.

A typical comment from examinees leaving the exam is, "I could not decide between the last two choices."

The positive side of that problem is eliminating two of the four choices.

### Pick the winning side

The most common choice pattern is the "two-two" pattern – two choices state that the plaintiff prevails, and two that the defendant prevails.

The best approach for this type of question is to rely on your knowledge of the law or instinctive feeling to which conclusion is correct.

In a question with two choices on one side and two on the other side of a court's decision, first, pick a choice on the side you think should prevail.

Distinguish between the explanations following this conclusion and pick the choice that best justifies it.

### Distance between choices on the other side

If the justifications following the conclusion for the side you chose seem indistinguishable, look at the explanations for the choices on the other side.

If the reasons for the choices on the other side are readily distinguishable, and one appears reasonable and the other incorrect, reconsider your initial conclusion.

Remember, the examiner is required to provide a distinguishable reason why one explanation of a general conclusion is correct, and the other is wrong.

That obligation does not exist if the general conclusion itself is incorrect.

Suppose choices (A) and (B) on one side look correct; that is, they are reasonable and consistent with the fact pattern. One of the choices with the opposite conclusion, answer (C), seems incorrect or inconsistent with the facts, and answer (D) with the same general conclusion sounds reasonable. From a strictly technical viewpoint, the best choice is answer (D).

### Questions based upon a common fact pattern

There are several instances where two or more questions are based on the same facts.

Look at the second question's wording to guide the first question's correct answer. When asked to assume an answer to a first question from a fact pattern to answer the second question, the probability is high that the answer to the first question follows that assumption.

For example, if the first question has two choices beginning with "P prevails" and two with "D prevails," and the second question starts with "If P prevails," it is likely one of the "P prevails" choices is correct for the first question. If you picked "D prevails," think carefully before selecting it as the final answer.

### Multiple true/false issues

In addition to true/false questions, the exam sometimes states three propositions in the root of the question and tests characteristics of those propositions in the call of the question.

The choices list various combinations of propositions.

The difference between this type of question and the double true/false question is that only four of the eight possible combinations fit into the options. It is possible to answer correctly even if you are not sure of all propositions' truth or falsity but are sure of one.

### Correctly stated, but the inapplicable principle of law

The task of the examiners is to make the wrong choices look attractive. A creative way to accomplish this is to write a choice that impeccably states a rule of law that is not applicable because of facts in the root of the question.

For example, in a question where a person is an assignee, not a sublessee, one of the choices may correctly state the law for sublessees, but it is inapplicable to the fact pattern.

Therefore, these answer choices with inapplicable law can be confidently eliminated.

## "Because" questions

Conjunctions are commonly used in the answers. It is essential to understand their role in determining whether a choice is correct.

The word "because" connects a conclusion and the reason for that conclusion with the facts in the body of the question.

There are two requirements for a question using "because" to be correct:

    1) the conclusion must be correct,

    2) the reasoning must logically follow based upon facts in the question, and the statement which follows "because" must be legally correct.

If the "because" choice has the correct result for the wrong reason, it is incorrect.

## "If" questions

The conjunction "if" requires a much narrower focus than "because."

When a choice contains an "if," determine whether the entire statement is true, assuming that the proposition which follows the "if" is true.

There is no requirement that facts in the root of the question support the proposition following "if." There is no requirement for facts in the question to support the proposition that such a construction be reasonable.

## "Because" or "if" need not be exclusive

There is no requirement for the conclusion following "if" or "because" to be exclusive.

For example, if a master could be liable in tort under the doctrine of *respondeat superior* or because the master was *negligent*, a choice using "if" or "because" holding the master liable would be correct if it stated either reason, even though the master might be liable for the other reason.

## Exam tip for "because"

Notice that in an answer that would have been correct, the word "because" limits the facts you could consider to those in the body of the question containing specific facts.

The difference between the effect of "if" and "because" controls the answer.

Identify those limited situations (e.g., where the appropriate standard is strict liability) and distinguish them from those that are satisfactory (e.g., if the standard is negligence).

### "Only if" requires exclusivity

Sometimes the words "only if" are used to distinguish between the two "affirmed" choices to make one wrong.

When an option uses the words "only if," assume that the entire proposition is correct as long as the words following "only if" are true.

The critical difference, where "only if" is used, is that the proposition cannot be true except when the condition is true. If there is another reason for the same result to be reached, the choice is wrong.

### "Unless" questions

The conjunction "unless" has the same function as "only if," except that it precedes a negative exclusive condition instead of a positive exclusive condition.

It is essentially the mirror image of an "only if" choice.

For an option using "unless," reverse and substitute the words "only if" for "unless."

### Limiting words

Choices can be made incorrect with limiting words that require that a proposition be true in all circumstances or under no circumstances.

Examples of limiting words include *all*, *any*, *never*, *always*, *only*, *every*, and *plenary*.

*Notes for active learning*

## Making Correct Judgment Calls

### Applying the law to the facts

Most questions give a fact pattern and ask which choice draws the correct legal conclusion required by the call of the question.

The first skill required is to draw inferences from facts given to place the conduct described in the question in the appropriate legal category.

The second skill is to apply the appropriate legal rule to conduct in that category and choose the option which reaches the appropriate conclusion.

The process of drawing inferences from a fact pattern and placing conduct in an appropriate category often requires judgment.

### Bad judgment equals the wrong answer

To make the questions difficult, the examiners often place the conduct near the border of two different legal classifications.

Decide which side of the demarcation the conduct falls on. Inevitably, reasonable people can differ on these judgments.

If your judgment does not match the examiners, you will likely answer the question incorrectly, no matter how much law you know.

Mitigate this problem by reviewing released questions involving judgment calls where the examiners have published correct answers (i.e., their judgment call).

For example, a death occurring because the parties played Russian roulette is considered *depraved heart murder*, not *involuntary manslaughter*.

### Judgment calls happen

Difficult judgment calls occur several times on the exam, and you are likely to make some close judgment calls incorrectly.

While this adds to the frustrations of multiple-choice tests, it is part of the exam.

By narrowing judgment call questions to two choices and guessing, you will get approximately half of them correct.

You will not fail the exam solely because you were unlucky on judgment calls.

The examiners remove many judgment calls by procedural devices.

## The importance of procedure

The question may not ask what a jury should find on the facts.

The answer may be controlled by the procedural context of the criminal prosecution.

For example, it is given that the jury has found the defendant guilty of murder, and the only question on appeal is whether the judge should have granted a motion to dismiss at the end of hearing evidence. This is because a reasonable jury looking at the facts and inferences most favorable to the prosecution should not have found the defendant guilty of murder.

The same procedural issues exist when the question asks if a motion for summary judgment should be allowed or if the court should direct a verdict.

## Exam Tips and Suggestions

### Timing is everything

The time given to complete the exam is usually adequate if you practiced enough questions to improve speed and efficiency to the required level.

As you get closer to the test date, just doing practice questions is not enough.

You need to time your practice. Take previously released exams in two three-hour periods on the same day. Since these practice exams are approximately the same length as the exam, you will know if you have a timing problem.

If you do not practice under timed conditions, you risk exhausting time on the exam before answering all the questions.

Practice your timing under test-like conditions to know if the timing will be an issue. If you cannot complete the practice exam, you will have trouble with the exam.

If time is an issue, adjust your pace and continue practicing.

All questions do not require the same amount of time.

### An approach for when time is not an issue

If you can complete 100 questions in three hours, use this strategy. At the start of the exam, break the allotted time into 15-minute intervals and write them down.

Set an initial pace of 9 questions every fifteen minutes.

Check your progress at each 15-minute interval.

If you completed 18 questions in the first half-hour, 36 in the first hour, 72 in the first two hours, and 90 in the first two and a half hours, you are on target to complete the exam on time. At this pace, you should complete 100 questions in two hours and forty-six minutes.

This leaves 14 minutes to check the answer sheet, revisit troublesome questions, or use the time to go a little slower on the last questions when fatigue impairs acuity.

If you find that your careful pace is faster than the budgeted 9 questions every 15 minutes, work at a faster pace, but use the extra time on the more challenging questions or in rechecking your work at the end.

Do *not* change the original answer choice unless you have a specific reason.

It is unwise to leave the exam early.

### An approach for when time is an issue

During practice, continue answering questions to complete the section even after the time for self-paced exams has expired. Note which question you completed within the allocated time. Strive to complete the questions within the allotted time during your final exam prep.

If you learn from taking the practice test that you may not finish the questions in the allotted time on the actual exam, skip those questions with a long fact pattern followed by only one question. Keep your place on the answer sheet by skipping the row.

Return to those questions at the end and complete as many as time permits. Before turning your exam in, guess at the rest to reduce the number of random guesses.

Answer every question, even if you have not read the question, since wrong answers do *not* count against you.

### Difficult questions

If you do not know the answer, do not spend a disproportionate amount of time on it since each question counts the same. Mark it in the test booklet, make a shrewd guess within the budgeted time and come back if time allows.

Do *not* leave questions unanswered. No points are deducted for wrong answers.

### Minimize fatigue to maximize your score

The mental energy required to answer all the multiple-choice questions under stress produces fatigue (even with a lunch break).

Fatigue slows processing questions effectively and impairs reading comprehension. You may process questions more slowly at the end of each session and more quickly at the beginning before fatigue sets in.

Take at least two released exams under timed conditions to know how significantly fatigue affects your performance.

Be sure to arrive at the exam site on time. If necessary, stay at a nearby hotel rather than getting up early and risking a long drive the morning of the exam.

Relax during the lunch break and do not discuss the morning session with others.

You should know enough about your metabolism to eat the correct foods during the exam and reinforce appropriate caffeine levels if appropriate.

## Proofread the answer sheet

As you decide on each correct answer, circle the corresponding letter in the exam book, and mark the appropriate block on the answer sheet.

The answer sheet is the only document graded by the examiners.

At the pace of 9 questions per 15 minutes, about 14 minutes should remain. Spend that time proofreading the answer sheet. Verify the answers circled to be certain that you marked the appropriate block on the answers.

Ensure that there are no blanks, and no questions have two answers.

Do *not* use this time to change an answer already selected unless you have a particularly good reason to change it.

If you have erased, ensure the erasure is thorough, or the computer may reject the answer because it cannot distinguish between marked answers.

If you have time after proofreading, review the problematic questions, and re-think the answers chosen. However, even after careful thought, hesitate to change an answer.

Do not leave any section of the exam early; use the allotted time wisely.

## Intelligent preparation over a sustained period

There is no easy way to conquer an exam as challenging and comprehensive as the MBE, except through practice and an investment of time and effort well before the exam.

By diligently preparing, practicing questions, and intelligently assessing why questions were answered incorrectly, your skills for the exam will improve substantially.

Continue to improve those skills by following the advice given herein until reaching a proficiency level enabling you to pass the bar. This proficiency is accurately measured in multiple-choice format questions.

Some students will have to work harder to achieve the required proficiency.

The tools are in this study guide, and any law school graduate can be successful in passing the bar if they invest the required time and effort to be prepared.

*Notes for active learning*

## Essay Preparation Strategies and Essay-Writing Suggestions

### Memorize the law

Do not make the mistake of waiting too long before memorizing the governing law. Start learning the governing law early to be better prepared and pass the exam.

Memorize essential principles and focus on highly tested governing law.

### Focus on the highly tested essay rules

Do not treat all subjects the same when you prepare for the essay portion of the exam.

Some governing law topics are tested more than others. It is crucial to focus on the highly tested topics (e.g., torts, contracts. property, civil procedure).

Know and apply enough governing laws to pass the bar – focus on commonly tested governing laws (e.g., negligence) provided in this book.

### Practice writing essay answers each week

Practicing is crucial to a high score on essays. Practice regularly and avoid procrastination for this essential component of bar prep.

Incorporate practicing essay writing into your exam study schedule. To reduce procrastination, schedule time for writing practice essays each week.

For the MPT, practice by drafting full MPTs. Most examinees procrastinate on preparing for the MPT; there is nothing to memorize.

Do not make the *fatal mistake* of not practicing. The MPT portion is worth 20% of the UBE score.

Know the format and *practice that format to* increase your UBE score. This practice will increase your score and the probability of passing the bar.

### Add one essay-specific subject each week

The Multistate Essay Exam (MEE) subjects include the 7 MBE subjects plus the 5 subjects of Business Associations (Agency, Partnerships, Corporations, and LLCs), Conflict of Laws, Family Law, Trusts and Estates, and Secured Transactions (UCC Article 9).

Combine highly tested subjects (e.g., torts) with less-tested subjects (e.g., secured transactions) and complex topics (e.g., contracts) with easier topics (e.g., business associations).

From preparation, know which subjects you struggle with and require a focused effort to master the essential governing law.

### Make it easy for the grader to award points

Your answer to a question will probably be read in less than five minutes by a grader with a checklist to find that you have seen the issues and discussed them intelligently. Writing organized and clear answers makes it easy for the essay grader to award points.

Use headings for each of the major issues.

If the question suggests a structure for the answer because it is divided into parts or because the facts present a series of discrete issues, use the structure of the question, which is probably the structure of the checklist.

Use the IRAC method for the essay questions: state the issue, state the Rule. Apply the rule to the facts and conclude. IRAC seems simple, but following this approach makes it easier for the grader to know that you identified and addressed every issue and applied the law to the facts given.

IRAC results in more points during the exam.

Do not spend time trying to formulate eloquent issue statements. The question often outlines the issues, so an eloquent issue statement is redundant, and issue statements do not earn extra points.

Many examinees spend too much time developing an impressive issue statement and omit other essentials of their analysis (e.g., truncated analysis section).

An issue statement "Torts" or "Is the defendant liable for negligence?" is enough.

Do not waste time arguing both sides. There are no "two sides" for many essays to argue on bar essays because these are not law school essays.

Apply the law to facts and conclude unless asserting each party has good arguments.

### Conclusion for each essay question

Points will be lost unless you conclude for each issue identified in the facts or are asked to address it in the call of the question.

Use caution starting the essay with the conclusion unless confident it is correct.

Many sample answers provided by the National Conference of Bar Examiners start with a definite and strong conclusion. Use caution to start with a conclusion unless confident (e.g., NCBE sample responses) your conclusion is correct.

Starting with a conclusion that is not correct draws attention to an incorrect conclusion at the start, which may influence the grader disproportionality. The grader may lose faith in your answer from the onset, and it is advisable to have a neutral heading rather than a firm conclusion that is wrong.

## Tips for an easy-to-read essay

Use paragraph breaks between the Issue, Rule, Analysis, and Conclusion. Paragraph break makes it easy for the grader to read and score your essays. Additionally, this approach makes the answer appear longer and more complete.

Emphasize keywords and phrases. Underline key phrases so the grader notices that you addressed the governing law and applied it to the facts given.

After graders score several essays on the same topic, they scan essays for specific phrases that they expect to locate within a complete essay.

## Think before you write

Read each question carefully to understand the facts and their necessary implications thoroughly and accurately.

After skimming the question, spend time on the focus line at the end of the question. Review the facts with the call of the question in mental focus.

Write a short outline of the issues raised. Outline in your mind the issues; state to yourself the tentative conclusions; test each conclusion from the standpoints of law and common sense; revise, as necessary.

Decide on a logical, orderly, and convincing arrangement for the response. Until then, you are not ready to write the answer.

Of the thirty-six minutes allotted to each essay, spend 15 minutes on issue spotting and organization and about twenty minutes writing the answer.

## The ability to think and communicate like a lawyer

The Board knows that you have completed law school, under competent instructors, and have passed law school exams. The bar does not challenge the results of your law school courses.

The exam tests the ability to apply what you have learned to facts that might arise in practice and which, in some instances, involve several fields of law. The value of an answer depends not only on the correctness of the conclusions but on displaying essential legal principles and thinking like a lawyer.

Conclude on each issue presented. If a conclusion is derived from fuzzy facts, construct a well-reasoned argument supporting your conclusion to receive full credit regardless of if you conclude the same as the examiners.

# Law Essentials: Contracts

If the correct answer depends on a provision of substantive law, which you are not familiar with, you can obtain a passing answer to the question by reaching a well-reasoned conclusion applying general law principles.

Do not try to limit the question to a particular subject area. Many questions combine traditional subjects, and you must be prepared to answer the question applying principles you learned across various subjects.

### Do not restate the facts

The examiners know the facts; there is no time to waste. Do not restate the facts but use them to apply and integrate legal principles in writing the essay.

Do not fight the facts, particularly the focus line of the question.

For example, if the facts state that A executed a valid will, write about valid wills. If the question asks you to argue on behalf of A, do not argue on behalf of B because B has a prevailing argument. However, raise potential arguments which could be made on behalf of B and counter them in arguing on behalf of A.

### Do not state abstract or irrelevant propositions of law

It is usually undesirable to begin an answer with a legal proposition. If the proposition is applicable, it will be more appropriate later to indicate the reason for your conclusion. If it is not applicable, do not state a surplus fact or legal principle.

Although it is seldom necessary to state an applicable rule of law in detail, make a sufficient reference to it so that the examiner appreciates your knowledge of the principle and conditions when it applies.

Do not, by speculating on different facts, nor in other ways, work into your answer some point of law with which you happen to be familiar, but which does not apply to the answer. Importantly, the examiners are not interested in knowing how many rules of law you know, but your ability to apply the applicable rules to the facts.

If the question says that A and B in the above hypothetical are unrelated, do not talk about the results which would occur if they were husband and wife.

Use the principles of law applicable to the call of the question and the facts. You must state the principles of applicable law to demonstrate to the examiner that you know the elements of the rule and how they apply to these facts.

For example, if the facts said that A transferred to B (a non-relative) the money necessary for B to purchase Blackacre from C and asks who owns Blackacre, you would say, "Since A furnished the consideration for the purchase of Blackacre and B took the title to the property in their name, B holds title to Blackacre in a resulting trust for A.

Do not detail the black letter law of resulting trusts since you have shown your knowledge by properly applying the facts to the law of resulting trusts.

Do not fight the facts and address a contrary fact not presented. The examiners may take points away if you make that mistake because you are not focused on the issues presented.

### Discuss all the issues raised

A grasp of all the issues is essential.

For example, if there are three issues in a question, a discussion of only one issue, no matter how masterly, if coupled with omitting the others, could not result in 100% credit. It would probably result in a score of 33%.

The exam includes many issues in most questions so it can be graded mechanically. This maintains consistency across a group of several graders for each exam question.

The grader has a checklist of issues and awards most points for the examinee that identifies issues and intelligently discusses each.

Failure to see and discuss enough issues intelligently is probably the biggest reason for failure on the essay portion of the exam.

### Methods for finding all issues

Use all the facts presented. Failure to discuss facts probably means that you missed important issues.

If you must decide in the early part of the question (e.g., does the court have jurisdiction) and you decide that issue so the remaining facts become irrelevant, make an alternative assumption ("If the court does have jurisdiction") and answer the question in the alternative using facts which would otherwise be irrelevant.

Do not avoid issues because you are not sure of the substantive law. If the examiners stated that X's nephew helped X escape after a crime, discuss the nephew's status as an accessory after the fact. If you do not know whether he is a close enough relative to be exempt under the statute, answer this issue by making alternative assumptions.

### Indicators requiring alternative arguments

*Ambiguous terms* – if there are words in the fact pattern that are neutral or ambiguous such as "put up," the examiners look for possible interpretations of these terms.

*Language in quotes* – language placed in quotes is almost always ambiguous and must be construed as part of the answer.

## Avoid ambiguous, rambling statements and verbosity

Generally, do not use compound sentences. Two separate sentences are preferred.

Complex sentences are particularly useful to apply the facts of the question to the applicable principle of law.

For example, in the previous resulting trust hypothetical, write, "Since B purchased Blackacre and took title in their name with money furnished by A, A holds title to Blackacre in a resulting trust, even if B has not signed a memorandum."

## Avoid undue repetition

If the same principle of law and conclusion apply to two parts of an answer, state it once in detail, and refer back for the second part.

For example, if you have discussed A's liability and now must discuss B's liability, say, "B is also guilty of murder for the same reasons as A. (see discussion above)."

## Avoid slang and colloquialism

The examiners judge your formal writing style.

If the examiner shows humor with names and events, do not show your sense of humor.

Use the standard abbreviations:

P for Plaintiff

D for Defendant

K for Contract

BFP for *Bona Fide* purchaser

## Write legibly and coherently

Printing is usually easier to read than handwriting.

Use all the pages, and do not crowd your answer.

Plan your answer so that you do not have to use inserts and arrows.

## Timing strategies

On the MEE, you must complete six equally weighted essay questions in three hours; an average of 30 minutes per question.

You have flexibility with time limitations as questions are not of the same difficulty.

There are two absolute figures:

    spend no more than 45 minutes on any question,

    spend at least 20 minutes on each question.

Be careful about not going over the time limit on the first question because this will require a readjustment of your timing for the entire session. If you miss the deadlines, re-divide your remaining time so that you will have an equal amount of time on each question.

If you go over by 15 minutes a question, do not allocate 30 minutes for other questions.

## Stay focused

Do not start by reading the entire exam. Answer the questions in order and do not consider more than one question at a time.

After answering, put it out of your mind and not worry about your response. Keep your mind clear to focus on the next question.

Proofread your answers as time permits.

## Law school essay grading matrix

An "A" answer is an outstanding response. It correctly and fully identifies dispositive issues and sub-issues raised by the question. The answer states the applicable legal rules and sub-rules with precision. It analyzes the question thoroughly with the applicable rules and explores alternative analysis where appropriate. It applies the law to the facts to conclude and is not cluttered by irrelevant matters. An "A" answer demonstrates an objectively superior mastering of the subject. An answer is not an "A" answer simply because it is better than most students' answers.

A "B" answer is a good response. It presents the four components of a good answer (issues, rules, analysis & application, and conclusion), but it does so in a way that could be improved. For example, it may be that not all critical issues have been spotted, or the issues are not presented clearly. The statement of legal rules captures that basic law but may not develop the law's complexities or nuances. The analysis is competent but lacks subtlety and may be somewhat simplistic or conclusory.

A "C" answer is a minimally competent response. It contains the four components of a good answer (issues, rules, analysis & application, and conclusion) but may not distinguish them. Perhaps only some issues have been identified while others are missed. The rules of law lack completeness or accuracy. The analysis and application may be shallow and conclusory. Conclusions may be questionable and not well-defended.

A "D" answer lacks basic components. It may identify the wrong issues or none. Rules are stated incorrectly. The analysis is conclusory or absent. The law is not applied to the facts coherently. Conclusions are unsupported or missing. The response exhibits a lack of knowledge of legal issues and rules or demonstrates an inability to engage in legal analysis.

*Best wishes with your preparation!*

# Appendix

## Overview of American Law

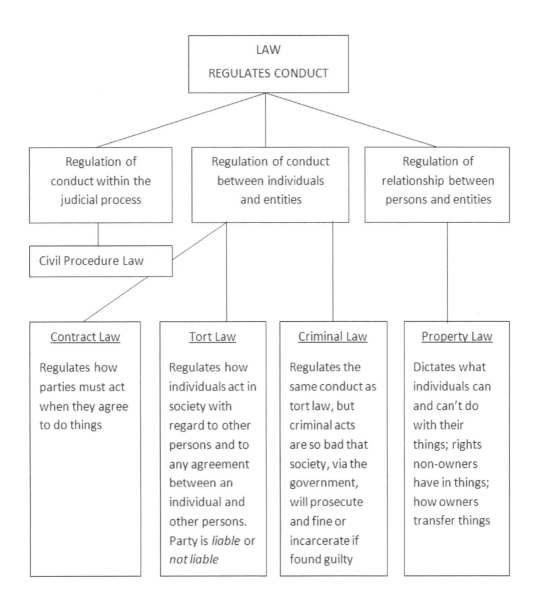

## U.S. Court Systems – Federal and State Courts

There are two kinds of courts in the USA – federal courts and state courts.

Federal courts are established under the U.S. Constitution by Congress to decide disputes involving the Constitution and laws passed by Congress. A state establishes state and local courts (within states, local courts are established by cities, counties, and other municipalities).

### Jurisdiction of federal and state courts

The differences between federal courts and state courts are defined by jurisdiction.[1] Jurisdiction refers to the kinds of cases that a particular court is authorized to hear and adjudicate (i.e., the pronouncement of a legally binding judgment upon the parties to the dispute).

Federal court jurisdiction is limited to the types of cases listed in the Constitution and specifically provided by Congress. For the most part, federal courts only hear:

- cases in which the United States is a party[2];
- cases involving violations of the U.S. Constitution or federal laws (under federal-question jurisdiction[3]);
- cases between citizens of different states if the amount in controversy *exceeds* $75,000 (under diversity jurisdiction[4]); and
- bankruptcy, copyright, patent, and maritime law cases.

State courts, in contrast, have broad jurisdiction, so the cases individual citizens are likely to be involved in (e.g., robberies, traffic violations, contracts, and family disputes) are usually heard and decided in state courts. The only cases state courts are not allowed to hear are lawsuits against the United States and those involving certain specific federal laws: criminal, antitrust, bankruptcy, patent, copyright, and some maritime law cases.

In many cases, both federal and state courts have jurisdiction whereby the plaintiff (i.e., the party initiating the suit) can choose whether to file their claim in state or federal court.

Criminal cases involving federal laws can be tried only in federal court, but most criminal cases involve violations of state law and are tried in state court. Robbery is a crime, but what law makes it is a crime? Except for certain exceptions, state laws, not federal laws, make robbery a crime. There are only a few federal laws about robbery, such as the law that makes it a federal crime to rob a bank whose deposits are insured by a federal agency. Examples of other federal crimes are the transport of illegal drugs into the country or across state lines and using the U.S. mail system to defraud consumers.

Crimes committed on federal property (e.g., national parks or military reservations) are prosecuted in federal court.

Federal courts may hear cases concerning state laws if the issue is whether the state law violates the federal Constitution. Suppose a state law forbids slaughtering animals outside of certain limited areas. A neighborhood association brings a case in state court against a defendant who sacrifices chickens in their backyard. When the court issues an order (i.e., an injunction[5]) forbidding the defendant from further sacrifices, the defendant challenges the state law in federal court as an unconstitutional infringement of religious freedom.

Some conduct is illegal under both federal and state laws. For example, federal laws prohibit employment discrimination, and the states have added additional legal restrictions. A person can file their claim in either federal or state court under federal law or federal and state laws. A case that only involves a state law can be brought only in state court.

Appeals for review of actions by federal administrative agencies are federal civil cases.

For example, if the Environmental Protection Agency, over the objection of area residents, issued a permit to a paper mill to discharge water used in its milling process into the Scenic River, the residents may appeal and have the federal court of appeals review the agency's decision.

---

[1] *jurisdiction* – 1) the legal authority of a court to hear and decide specific types of case; 2) the geographic area over which the court has the authority to decide cases.

[2] *parties* – the plaintiff and the defendant in a lawsuit.

[3] *federal-question jurisdiction* – the federal district courts' authorization to hear and decide cases arising under the Constitution, laws, or treaties of the United States.

[4] *diversity jurisdiction* – the federal district courts' authority to hear and decide civil cases involving plaintiffs and defendants who are citizens of different states (or U.S. citizens and foreign nationals) and meet specific statutory requirements.

[5] *injunction* – a judge's order that a party takes or refrain from taking a particular action. An injunction may be preliminary until the outcome of a case is determined or permanent.

## Organization of the federal courts

Congress has divided the country into 94 federal judicial districts, with each having a U.S. district court. The U.S. district courts are the federal trial courts -- where federal cases are tried, witnesses testify, and juries serve.

Each district has a U.S. bankruptcy court, which is part of the district court that administers the U.S. bankruptcy laws.

Congress uses state boundaries to help define the districts. Some districts cover an entire state, like Idaho. Other districts cover just part of a state, like the Northern District of California. Congress placed each of the ninety-four districts in one of twelve regional circuits whereby each circuit has a court of appeals. The losing party can petition the court of appeals to review the case to determine if the district judge applied the law correctly.

There is a U.S. Court of Appeals for the Federal Circuit, whose jurisdiction is defined by subject matter rather than geography. It hears appeals from certain courts and agencies, such as the U.S. Court of International Trade, the U.S. Court of Federal Claims, and the U.S. Patent and Trademark Office, and certain types of cases from the district courts (mainly lawsuits claiming that patents have been infringed).

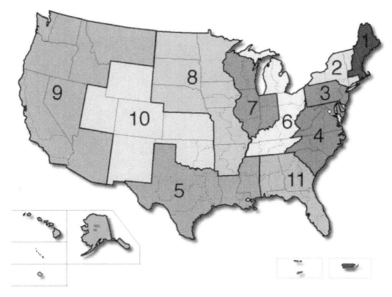

Twelve regional federal circuits

The Supreme Court in Washington, D.C., is the highest court in the nation. The losing party can petition in a case in the court of appeals (or, sometimes, in a state supreme court), can petition the Supreme Court to hear an appeal.

Unlike a court of appeals, the Supreme Court does not have to hear the case. The Supreme Court hears only a small percentage of the cases it is asked to review.

*Notes for active learning*

## How Civil Cases Move Through the Federal Courts

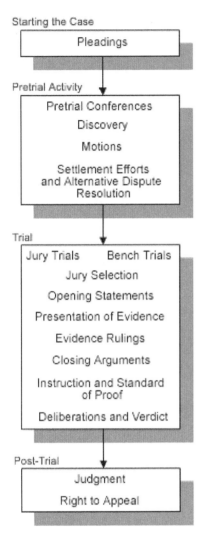

A federal civil case begins when a person, or their legal representative, files a paper with the clerk of the court that asserts another person's wrongful act injured the person. In legal terminology, the plaintiff files a *complaint* against the defendant.

The defendant files an *answer* to the complaint. These written statements of the party's positions are called pleadings. In some circumstances, the defendant may file a *motion* instead of an answer; the motion asks the court to take some action, such as dismiss the case or require the plaintiff to explain more clearly what the lawsuit is about.

### Jury trials

In a jury trial, the jury decides what happened, and to apply the legal standards, the judge tells them to apply to reach a verdict. The plaintiff presents evidence supporting its view of the case, and the defendant presents evidence rebutting the plaintiff's evidence or supporting its view of the case. From these presentations, the jury must decide what happened and applied the law to those facts.

The jury never decides what law applies to the case; that is the role of the judge. For example, in a discrimination case where the plaintiff alleged that their workplace was hostile, the judge tells the jury the legal standard for a hostile environment.

The jury would have to decide whether the plaintiff's description of events was true and whether those events met the legal standard. A trial jury, or petit jury, may consist of six to twelve jurors in a civil case.

## Bench trials

If the parties agree not to have a *jury trial* and leave the fact-finding to the judge, the trial is a *bench trial*. In bench and jury trials, the judge ensures the correct legal standards are followed.

In contrast to a jury trial, the judge decides the facts and renders the verdict in a *bench trial*.

For example, in a discrimination case in which the plaintiff alleged a hostile environment, the judge would determine the legal standard for a hostile environment and decide whether the plaintiff's description of events was true and whether those events met the legal standard.

Some kinds of cases always have bench trials. For example, there is never a jury trial if the plaintiff is seeking an injunction, an order from the judge that the defendant does, or stop doing something, as opposed to monetary damages.

Some statutes provide that a judge must decide the facts in certain types of cases.

## Jury selection

A jury trial begins with the selection of jurors. Citizens are selected for jury service through a process set out in laws passed by Congress and in the federal rules of procedure.

First, citizens are called to court to be available to serve on juries. These citizens are selected at random from sources, in most districts, lists of registered voters, which may be augmented by other sources, such as lists of licensed drivers in the judicial district.

The judge and the lawyers choose who will serve on the jury.

To choose the jurors, the judge and sometimes the lawyers ask prospective jurors questions to determine if they will decide the case fairly, a process known as *voir dire*.

The lawyers may request that the judge excuse jurors they think may not be impartial, such as those who know a party in the case or who have had an experience that might make them favor one side over the other. These requests for rejecting jurors are *challenges for cause*.

The lawyers may request that the judge excuse a certain number of jurors without reason; these requests are *peremptory challenges*.

## Instructions and standard of proof

Following the closing arguments, the judge gives instructions to the jury, explaining the relevant law, how the law applies to the case, and what questions the jury must decide.

How sure do jurors have to be before they reach a verdict? One important instruction the judge gives the jury is the standard of proof they must follow in deciding the case.

The courts, through their decisions, and Congress, through statutes, have established standards by which facts must be proven in criminal and civil cases.

In civil cases, to decide for the plaintiff, the jury must determine by a *preponderance of the evidence* that the defendant failed to perform a legal duty and violated the plaintiff's rights. A preponderance of the evidence means that, based on the evidence, the evidence favors the plaintiff more (even if only slightly) than it favors the defendant.

If the evidence in favor of the plaintiff could be placed on one side of a scale and that in favor of the defendant on the other, the plaintiff would win if the evidence in favor of the plaintiff was heavy enough to tip the scale. If the two sides were even, or if the scale tipped for the defendant, the defendant would win.

## Judgment

In civil cases, if the jury (or judge) decides in favor of the plaintiff, the result usually is that the defendant must pay the plaintiff money or damages. The judge orders the defendant to pay the decided amount. Sometimes the defendant is ordered to take some specific action that will restore the plaintiff's rights. If the defendant wins the case, there is nothing more the trial court needs to do as the case is disposed of and the defendant is held not liable.

## Right to appeal

The losing party in a federal civil case has a right to appeal the verdict to the U.S. court of appeals (i.e., Federal Circuit Courts) and ask the court to review the case to determine whether the trial was conducted properly. The losing party in the state trial court has a right to appeal the verdict to the state court of appeal.

The grounds for appeal usually are that the federal district (or state) judge made an error, either in the procedure (e.g., admitting improper evidence) or interpreting the law. The government may appeal in civil cases, as any other party may. Neither party may appeal if there was no trial -- parties settled their civil case out of court.

*Notes for active learning*

*Appendix: How Criminal Cases Move Through the Federal Courts*

## How Criminal Cases Move Through the Federal Courts

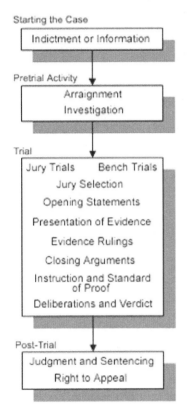

### Indictment or information

A criminal case formally begins with an indictment or information, which is a formal accusation that a person committed a crime.

An indictment may be obtained when a lawyer (i.e., prosecutor) for the executive branch of the U.S. government (i.e., U.S. attorney or assistant U.S. attorney) present evidence to a federal grand jury that, according to the government, indicates a person committed a crime.

The U.S. attorney tries to convince the grand jury that there is enough evidence to show that the person probably committed the crime and should be formally accused. If the grand jury agrees, it issues an indictment.

A grand jury is different from a trial jury or petit jury.

A grand jury determines whether the person may be tried for a crime; a petit jury listens to the evidence presented at the trial and determines whether the defendant is guilty.

*Petit* is French for "small"; petit juries usually consist of twelve jurors in criminal cases.

*Grand* is French for "large"; grand juries have from sixteen to twenty-three jurors.

Grand jury indictments are most often used for *felonies* (i.e., punishable by imprisonment of more than a year or by death) such as bank robberies or sales of illegal drugs.

Grand jury indictments are not necessary to prosecute *misdemeanors* (i.e., less serious than a felony but more serious than an infraction) and are necessary for felonies.

For lesser crimes, the U.S. attorney issues an *information* that substitutes for an indictment. For example, speeding on a highway in a national park is a misdemeanor.

An information is used when a defendant waives an indictment by a grand jury.

## Arraignment

After the grand jury issues the indictment, the accused (i.e., defendant) is summoned to court or arrested (if not already in custody). The next step is an arraignment, a proceeding in which the defendant is brought before a judge, told of the charges they are accused of, and asked to plead guilty or not guilty. If the defendant's plea is guilty, a time is set for the defendant to return to court to be sentenced.

If the defendant pleads "not guilty," the time is set for the trial.

A defendant may enter a plea bargain with the prosecution--usually by agreeing to plead guilty to some but not all charges or lesser charges. The prosecution drops the remaining charges.

About nine out of ten defendants in criminal cases plead guilty.

## Investigation

In a criminal case, a defense lawyer conducts a thorough investigation before trial, interviewing witnesses, visiting the crime scene, and examining physical evidence. An important part of this investigation is determining whether the evidence the government plans to use to prove its case was obtained legally.

The Fourth Amendment to the Constitution forbids unreasonable searches and seizures. To enforce this protection, the Supreme Court has decided that illegally seized evidence cannot be used at trial for most purposes.

For example, if the police seize evidence from a defendant's home without a search warrant, the lawyer for the defendant can ask the court to exclude the evidence from use at trial. The court holds a hearing to determine whether the search was unreasonable.

If the court rules that key evidence was seized illegally and cannot be used, the government often drops the charges against the defendant.

If the government has a strong case and the court ruled that the evidence was obtained legally, the defendant may decide to plead guilty rather than go to trial, where a conviction is likely.

## Deliberations and verdict

After receiving its instructions from the judge, the jury retires to the jury room to discuss the evidence and reach a verdict (a decision on the factual issues). A criminal jury verdict must be unanimous; all jurors must agree that the defendant is guilty or not guilty.

If the jurors cannot agree, the judge declares a mistrial, and the prosecutor must decide whether to ask the court to dismiss the case or have it presented to another jury.

## Judgment and sentencing

In federal criminal cases, if the jury (or judge, if there is no jury) decides that the defendant is guilty, the judge sets a date for a sentencing hearing. In federal criminal cases, the jury does not decide whether the defendant will go to prison or for how long; the judge does.

In federal death penalty cases, the jury does decide whether the defendant will receive a death sentence. Sentencing statutes passed by Congress control the judge's sentencing decision. Additionally, judges use Sentencing Guidelines, issued by the U.S. Sentencing Commission, as a source of advice as to the proper sentence. The guidelines consider the nature of the offense and the offender's criminal history.

A presentence report, prepared by one of the court's probation officers, provides the judge with information about the offender and the offense, including the sentence recommended by the guidelines. After determining the sentence, the judge signs a judgment, including the plea, the verdict, and sentence.

## Right to appeal

A defendant who is found guilty in a federal criminal trial has a right to appeal the decision to the U.S. court of appeals, that is, ask the court of appeals to review the case to determine whether the trial was conducted properly. The grounds for appeal are usually that the district judge is said to have made an error, either in a procedure (admitting improper evidence, for example) or interpreting the law.

A defendant who pled guilty may not appeal the conviction.

A defendant who pled guilty may have the right to appeal their sentence.

The government may not appeal if a defendant in a criminal case is found not guilty because the Double Jeopardy Clause of the Fifth Amendment to the Constitution provides that no person shall "be twice put in jeopardy of life or limb" for the same offense.

This reflects society's belief that, even if a subsequent trial might finally find a defendant guilty, it is not proper for the government to harass an acquitted defendant through repeated retrials.

However, the government may sometimes appeal a sentence.

*Notes for active learning*

# How Civil and Criminal Appeals Move Through the Federal Courts

- Assignment of Judges
- Alternative Dispute Resolution (ADR)
- Review of Lower Court Decision
- Oral Argument
- Decision
- The Supreme Court of the United States

### Assignment of judges

The courts of appeals usually assign cases to a panel of three judges. The panel decides the case for the entire court. Sometimes, when the parties request it or a question of unusual importance, the judges on the appeals court assemble *en banc* (a rare event).

### Review of a lower court decision

In making its decision, the panel reviews key parts of the record. The record consists of the documents filed in the case at trial and the transcript of the trial proceedings. The panel learns about the lawyers' legal arguments from the lawyers' briefs.

Briefs are written documents that each side submits to explain its case and tell why the court should decide in its favor.

### Oral argument

If the court permits oral argument, the lawyers for each side have a limited amount of time (typically between 15 to 30 minutes) to argue (i.e., advocate and explain) their case to the judges (or justices at the highest court in the jurisdiction) in a formal courtroom session. The judges (or justices for the highest court in the jurisdiction) frequently question the attorneys about the relevant law as it applies to the facts and issues in the case before them.

A court of appeals differs from the federal trial courts. There are no jurors, witnesses, or court reporters. The lawyers for each side, but not the parties, are usually present in the courtroom.

### Decision

After the submission of briefs and oral arguments, the judges discuss the case privately, consider relevant *precedents* (court decisions from higher courts in prior cases with similar facts and legal issues), and reach a decision. Courts are required to follow precedents.

For example, a U.S. court of appeals must follow the U.S. Supreme Court's decisions; a district court must follow the decisions of the U.S. Supreme Court and the decisions of the court of appeals of its circuit.

Courts are influenced by decisions they are not required to follow, such as the decisions of other circuits. Courts follow precedent unless they set forth reasons for the diversion.

At least two of the three judges on the panel must agree on a decision. One judge who agrees with the decision is chosen to write an opinion, which announces and explains the decision.

If a judge on the panel disagrees with the majority's opinion, the judge may write a dissent, giving reasons for disagreeing.

Many appellate opinions are published in books of opinions, called reporters. The opinions are read carefully by other judges and lawyers looking for precedents to guide them in their cases.

The accumulated judicial opinions make up a body of law known as *case law*, which is usually an accurate predictor of how future cases will be decided.

For decisions that the judges believe are important to the parties and contribute little to the law, the appeals courts frequently use short, unsigned opinions that often are not published.

If the court of appeals decides that the trial judge incorrectly interpreted the law or followed incorrect procedures, it reverses the district court's decision.

For example, the court of appeals could hold that the district judge allowed the jury to base its decision on evidence that never should have been admitted, and thus the defendant cannot be guilty.

Most of the time, courts of appeals uphold, rather than the reverse, district court decisions.

Sometimes when a higher court reverses the decision of the district court, it sends the case back (i.e., *remand* the case) to the lower court for another trial.

For example, *Miranda v. Arizona* case (1966), the Supreme Court ruled 5-4 that Ernesto Miranda's confession could not be used as evidence because he had not been advised of his right to remain silent or of his right to have a lawyer present during questioning.

However, the government did have other evidence against him. The case was remanded for a new trial, in which the improperly obtained confession was not used as evidence, but the other evidence convicted Miranda.

### The Supreme Court of the United States

The Supreme Court is the highest in the nation. It is a different kind of appeals court; its major function is not correcting errors made by trial judges but clarifying the law in cases of national importance or when lower courts disagree about interpreting the Constitution or federal laws.

The Supreme Court does not have to hear every case that it is asked to review. Each year, losing parties ask the Supreme Court to review about 8,000 cases.

Almost all cases come to the Court as a *petition for writ of certiorari*. The court selects only about 80 to 120 of the most significant cases to review with oral arguments.

Supreme Court decisions establish a precedent for interpreting the Constitution and federal laws; holdings that state and federal courts must follow.

The power of judicial review makes the Supreme Court's role in our government vital. Judicial review is the power of a court when deciding a case to declare that a law passed by a legislature or action by the executive branch is invalid because it is inconsistent with the Constitution.

Although district courts, courts of appeals, and state courts can exercise the power of judicial review, their decisions about federal law are always subject, on appeal, to review by the Supreme Court.

When the Supreme Court declares a law unconstitutional, its decision can only be overruled by a later decision of the Supreme Court or Amendment to the Constitution.

Seven of the twenty-seven Amendments to the Constitution have invalidated the decisions of the Supreme Court. However, most Supreme Court cases do not concern the constitutionality of laws, but the interpretation of laws passed by Congress.

Although Congress has steadily increased the number of district and appeals court judges over the years, the Supreme Court has remained the same size since 1869. It consists of a Chief Justice and eight associate justices.

Like the federal court of appeals and federal district judges, the Supreme Court justices are appointed by the President with the Senate's *advice and consent*.

Unlike the judges in the courts of appeals, Supreme Court justices never sit on panels. Absent recusal, nine justices hear cases, and a majority ruling decides cases.

The Supreme Court begins its annual session, or term, on the first Monday of October. The term lasts until the Court has announced its decisions in cases where it has heard an argument that term—usually late June or early July.

During the term, the Court, sitting for two weeks at a time, hears oral arguments on Monday through Wednesday and holds private conferences to discuss the cases, reach decisions, and begin preparing the written opinions that explain its decisions.

Most decisions and opinions are released in the late spring and early summer.

## Standards of review for federal courts

| Standard of review | De novo | Clearly erroneous | Abuse of discretion |
|---|---|---|---|
| Type of decision under review | Question of the law | Question of fact | Discretionary action |
| Lower-court decision maker | Trial judge | Trial judge | Trial judge |
| Deference given to lower court | No deference | Substantial deference | Extreme deference |
| Party typically benefitted | Appellant | Appellee | Appellee |
| Definition | An appellate court reviews the legal question anew and independently, without regard to the conclusions reached by the trial court. "When de novo review is compelled, no form of appellate deference is acceptable." *Salve Regina College v. Russell*, (1991). | A finding is 'clearly erroneous' when although there is evidence to support it, the reviewing court on the entire evidence is left with the definite and firm conviction that a mistake has been committed. *United States v. United States Gypsum Co.*, (1948). "If the district court's account of the evidence is plausible in light of the record viewed in its entirety, the court of appeals may not reverse it even though convinced that had it been sitting as the trier of fact, it would have weighed the evidence differently. When there are two permissible views of the evidence, the factfinder's choice between them cannot be clearly erroneous." *Anderson v. Bessemer City*, (1985). | Generally, an abuse of discretion only occurs where no reasonable person could take the view adopted by the trial court. If reasonable persons could differ, no abuse of discretion can be found. *Harrington v. DeVito*, (7th Cir.1981). Under the abuse of discretion standard, a trial court's decision will not be disturbed unless the appellate court has a definite and firm conviction that the lower court made a clear error of judgment or exceeded the bounds of permissible choice in the circumstances. We will not alter a trial court's decision unless it can be shown that the court's decision was an arbitrary, capricious, whimsical, or manifestly unreasonable judgment. *Wright v. Abbott Laboratories, Inc.*, (10th Cir. 2001). |
| Examples | Motions for summary judgment, constitutional questions, statutory interpretation | Questions regarding who did what, where, and when; questions of intent and motive; questions of ultimate fact (such as negligence) | Rule 11 sanctions, attorney's fees, courtroom management, motions to compel, injunctions, and temporary restraining orders. |

## The Constitution of the United States (*a transcription*)

THE U.S. NATIONAL ARCHIVES & RECORDS ADMINISTRATION
www.archives.gov

The following text is a transcription of the Constitution as it was inscribed by Jacob Shallus on parchment (the document on display in the Rotunda at the National Archives Museum.) The spelling and punctuation reflect the original.

### The Constitution of the United States: A Transcription

*The following text is a transcription of the Constitution as it was inscribed by Jacob Shallus on parchment (displayed in the Rotunda at the National Archives Museum.) The authenticated text of the Constitution can be found on the website of the Government Printing Office.*

---

**We the People** of the United States, in Order to form a more perfect Union, establish Justice, insure domestic Tranquility, provide for the common defence, promote the general Welfare, and secure the Blessings of Liberty to ourselves and our Posterity, do ordain and establish this Constitution for the United States of America.

---

### Article. I

**Section. 1.**

All legislative Powers herein granted shall be vested in a Congress of the United States, which shall consist of a Senate and House of Representatives.

**Section. 2.**

The House of Representatives shall be composed of Members chosen every second Year by the People of the several States, and the Electors in each State shall have the Qualifications requisite for Electors of the most numerous Branch of the State Legislature.

No Person shall be a Representative who shall not have attained to the Age of twenty five Years, and been seven Years a Citizen of the United States, and who shall not, when elected, be an Inhabitant of that State in which he shall be chosen.

Representatives and direct Taxes shall be apportioned among the several States which may be included within this Union, according to their respective Numbers, which shall be determined by adding to the whole Number of free Persons, including those bound to Service for a Term of Years, and excluding Indians not taxed, three fifths of all other Persons. The actual Enumeration shall be made within three Years after the first Meeting of the Congress of the United States, and within every subsequent Term of ten Years, in such Manner as they shall by Law direct. The Number of Representatives shall not exceed one for every thirty Thousand, but each State shall have at Least one Representative; and until such enumeration shall be made, the State of New Hampshire shall be entitled to chuse three, Massachusetts eight, Rhode-Island and Providence

Plantations one, Connecticut five, New-York six, New Jersey four, Pennsylvania eight, Delaware one, Maryland six, Virginia ten, North Carolina five, South Carolina five, and Georgia three.

When vacancies happen in the Representation from any State, the Executive Authority thereof shall issue Writs of Election to fill such Vacancies.

The House of Representatives shall chuse their Speaker and other Officers; and shall have the sole Power of Impeachment.

**Section. 3.**

The Senate of the United States shall be composed of two Senators from each State, chosen by the Legislature thereof, for six Years; and each Senator shall have one Vote.

Immediately after they shall be assembled in Consequence of the first Election, they shall be divided as equally as may be into three Classes. The Seats of the Senators of the first Class shall be vacated at the Expiration of the second Year, of the second Class at the Expiration of the fourth Year, and of the third Class at the Expiration of the sixth Year, so that one third may be chosen every second Year; and if Vacancies happen by Resignation, or otherwise, during the Recess of the Legislature of any State, the Executive thereof may make temporary Appointments until the next Meeting of the Legislature, which shall then fill such Vacancies.

No Person shall be a Senator who shall not have attained to the Age of thirty Years, and been nine Years a Citizen of the United States, and who shall not, when elected, be an Inhabitant of that State for which he shall be chosen.

The Vice President of the United States shall be President of the Senate, but shall have no Vote, unless they be equally divided.

The Senate shall chuse their other Officers, and also a President pro tempore, in the Absence of the Vice President, or when he shall exercise the Office of President of the United States.

The Senate shall have the sole Power to try all Impeachments. When sitting for that Purpose, they shall be on Oath or Affirmation. When the President of the United States is tried, the Chief Justice shall preside: And no Person shall be convicted without the Concurrence of two thirds of the Members present.

Judgment in Cases of Impeachment shall not extend further than to removal from Office, and disqualification to hold and enjoy any Office of honor, Trust or Profit under the United States: but the Party convicted shall nevertheless be liable and subject to Indictment, Trial, Judgment and Punishment, according to Law.

**Section. 4.**

The Times, Places and Manner of holding Elections for Senators and Representatives, shall be prescribed in each State by the Legislature thereof; but the Congress may at any time by Law make or alter such Regulations, except as to the Places of chusing Senators.

The Congress shall assemble at least once in every Year, and such Meeting shall be on the first Monday in December, unless they shall by Law appoint a different Day.

**Section. 5.**

Each House shall be the Judge of the Elections, Returns and Qualifications of its own Members, and a Majority of each shall constitute a Quorum to do Business; but a smaller Number may adjourn from day to day, and may be authorized to compel the Attendance of absent Members, in such Manner, and under such Penalties as each House may provide.

Each House may determine the Rules of its Proceedings, punish its Members for disorderly Behaviour, and, with the Concurrence of two thirds, expel a Member.

Each House shall keep a Journal of its Proceedings, and from time to time publish the same, excepting such Parts as may in their Judgment require Secrecy; and the Yeas and Nays of the Members of either House on any question shall, at the Desire of one fifth of those Present, be entered on the Journal.

Neither House, during the Session of Congress, shall, without the Consent of the other, adjourn for more than three days, nor to any other Place than that in which the two Houses shall be sitting.

**Section. 6.**

The Senators and Representatives shall receive a Compensation for their Services, to be ascertained by Law, and paid out of the Treasury of the United States. They shall in all Cases, except Treason, Felony and Breach of the Peace, be privileged from Arrest during their Attendance at the Session of their respective Houses, and in going to and returning from the same; and for any Speech or Debate in either House, they shall not be questioned in any other Place.

No Senator or Representative shall, during the Time for which he was elected, be appointed to any civil Office under the Authority of the United States, which shall have been created, or the Emoluments whereof shall have been encreased during such time; and no Person holding any Office under the United States, shall be a Member of either House during his Continuance in Office.

**Section. 7.**

All Bills for raising Revenue shall originate in the House of Representatives; but the Senate may propose or concur with Amendments as on other Bills.

Every Bill which shall have passed the House of Representatives and the Senate, shall, before it become a Law, be presented to the President of the United States; If he approves he shall sign it, but if not he shall return it, with his Objections to that House in which it shall have originated, who shall enter the Objections at large on their Journal, and proceed to reconsider it. If after such Reconsideration two thirds of that House shall agree to pass the Bill, it shall be sent, together with the Objections, to the other House, by which it shall likewise be reconsidered, and if approved by two thirds of that House, it shall become a Law. But in all such Cases the Votes of both Houses shall be determined by yeas and Nays, and the Names of the Persons voting for and against the Bill shall be entered on the Journal of each House respectively. If any Bill shall not be returned by the President within ten Days (Sundays excepted) after it shall have been presented to him, the Same shall be a Law, in like Manner as if he had signed it, unless the Congress by their Adjournment prevent its Return, in which Case it shall not be a Law.

Every Order, Resolution, or Vote to which the Concurrence of the Senate and House of Representatives may be necessary (except on a question of Adjournment) shall be presented to the President of the United States; and before the Same shall take Effect, shall be approved by him, or being disapproved by him, shall be repassed by two thirds of the Senate and House of Representatives, according to the Rules and Limitations prescribed in the Case of a Bill.

**Section. 8.**

The Congress shall have Power To lay and collect Taxes, Duties, Imposts and Excises, to pay the Debts and provide for the common Defence and general Welfare of the United States; but all Duties, Imposts and Excises shall be uniform throughout the United States;

To borrow Money on the credit of the United States;

To regulate Commerce with foreign Nations, and among the several States, and with the Indian Tribes;

To establish an uniform Rule of Naturalization, and uniform Laws on the subject of Bankruptcies throughout the United States;

To coin Money, regulate the Value thereof, and of foreign Coin, and fix the Standard of Weights and Measures;

To provide for the Punishment of counterfeiting the Securities and current Coin of the United States;

To establish Post Offices and post Roads;

To promote the Progress of Science and useful Arts, by securing for limited Times to Authors and Inventors the exclusive Right to their respective Writings and Discoveries;

To constitute Tribunals inferior to the Supreme Court;

To define and punish Piracies and Felonies committed on the high Seas, and Offences against the Law of Nations;

To declare War, grant Letters of Marque and Reprisal, and make Rules concerning Captures on Land and Water;

To raise and support Armies, but no Appropriation of Money to that Use shall be for a longer Term than two Years;

To provide and maintain a Navy;

To make Rules for the Government and Regulation of the land and naval Forces;

To provide for calling forth the Militia to execute the Laws of the Union, suppress Insurrections and repel Invasions;

To provide for organizing, arming, and disciplining, the Militia, and for governing such Part of them as may be employed in the Service of the United States, reserving to the States respectively, the Appointment of the Officers, and the Authority of training the Militia according to the discipline prescribed by Congress;

To exercise exclusive Legislation in all Cases whatsoever, over such District (not exceeding ten Miles square) as may, by Cession of particular States, and the Acceptance of Congress, become the Seat of the Government of the United States, and to exercise like Authority over all Places purchased by the Consent of the Legislature of the State in which the Same shall be, for the Erection of Forts, Magazines, Arsenals, dock-Yards, and other needful Buildings;—And

To make all Laws which shall be necessary and proper for carrying into Execution the foregoing Powers, and all other Powers vested by this Constitution in the Government of the United States, or in any Department or Officer thereof.

**Section. 9.**

The Migration or Importation of such Persons as any of the States now existing shall think proper to admit, shall not be prohibited by the Congress prior to the Year one thousand eight hundred and eight, but a Tax or duty may be imposed on such Importation, not exceeding ten dollars for each Person.

The Privilege of the Writ of Habeas Corpus shall not be suspended, unless when in Cases of Rebellion or Invasion the public Safety may require it.

No Bill of Attainder or ex post facto Law shall be passed.

No Capitation, or other direct, Tax shall be laid, unless in Proportion to the Census or enumeration herein before directed to be taken.

No Tax or Duty shall be laid on Articles exported from any State.

No Preference shall be given by any Regulation of Commerce or Revenue to the Ports of one State over those of another: nor shall Vessels bound to, or from, one State, be obliged to enter, clear, or pay Duties in another.

No Money shall be drawn from the Treasury, but in Consequence of Appropriations made by Law; and a regular Statement and Account of the Receipts and Expenditures of all public Money shall be published from time to time.

No Title of Nobility shall be granted by the United States: And no Person holding any Office of Profit or Trust under them, shall, without the Consent of the Congress, accept of any present, Emolument, Office, or Title, of any kind whatever, from any King, Prince, or foreign State.

**Section. 10.**

No State shall enter into any Treaty, Alliance, or Confederation; grant Letters of Marque and Reprisal; coin Money; emit Bills of Credit; make any Thing but gold and silver Coin a Tender in Payment of Debts; pass any Bill of Attainder, ex post facto Law, or Law impairing the Obligation of Contracts, or grant any Title of Nobility.

No State shall, without the Consent of the Congress, lay any Imposts or Duties on Imports or Exports, except what may be absolutely necessary for executing it's inspection Laws: and the net

Produce of all Duties and Imposts, laid by any State on Imports or Exports, shall be for the Use of the Treasury of the United States; and all such Laws shall be subject to the Revision and Controul of the Congress.

No State shall, without the Consent of Congress, lay any Duty of Tonnage, keep Troops, or Ships of War in time of Peace, enter into any Agreement or Compact with another State, or with a foreign Power, or engage in War, unless actually invaded, or in such imminent Danger as will not admit of delay.

---

## Article. II

**Section. 1.**

The executive Power shall be vested in a President of the United States of America. He shall hold his Office during the Term of four Years, and, together with the Vice President, chosen for the same Term, be elected, as follows

Each State shall appoint, in such Manner as the Legislature thereof may direct, a Number of Electors, equal to the whole Number of Senators and Representatives to which the State may be entitled in the Congress: but no Senator or Representative, or Person holding an Office of Trust or Profit under the United States, shall be appointed an Elector.

The Electors shall meet in their respective States, and vote by Ballot for two Persons, of whom one at least shall not be an Inhabitant of the same State with themselves. And they shall make a List of all the Persons voted for, and of the Number of Votes for each; which List they shall sign and certify, and transmit sealed to the Seat of the Government of the United States, directed to the President of the Senate. The President of the Senate shall, in the Presence of the Senate and House of Representatives, open all the Certificates, and the Votes shall then be counted. The Person having the greatest Number of Votes shall be the President, if such Number be a Majority of the whole Number of Electors appointed; and if there be more than one who have such Majority, and have an equal Number of Votes, then the House of Representatives shall immediately chuse by Ballot one of them for President; and if no Person have a Majority, then from the five highest on the List the said House shall in like Manner chuse the President. But in chusing the President, the Votes shall be taken by States, the Representation from each State having one Vote; A quorum for this Purpose shall consist of a Member or Members from two thirds of the States, and a Majority of all the States shall be necessary to a Choice. In every Case, after the Choice of the President, the Person having the greatest Number of Votes of the Electors shall be the Vice President. But if there should remain two or more who have equal Votes, the Senate shall chuse from them by Ballot the Vice President.

The Congress may determine the Time of chusing the Electors, and the Day on which they shall give their Votes; which Day shall be the same throughout the United States.

No Person except a natural born Citizen, or a Citizen of the United States, at the time of the Adoption of this Constitution, shall be eligible to the Office of President; neither shall any Person be eligible to that Office who shall not have attained to the Age of thirty five Years, and been fourteen Years a Resident within the United States.

In Case of the Removal of the President from Office, or of his Death, Resignation, or Inability to discharge the Powers and Duties of the said Office, the Same shall devolve on the Vice President, and the Congress may by Law provide for the Case of Removal, Death, Resignation or Inability, both of the President and Vice President, declaring what Officer shall then act as President, and such Officer shall act accordingly, until the Disability be removed, or a President shall be elected.

The President shall, at stated Times, receive for his Services, a Compensation, which shall neither be encreased nor diminished during the Period for which he shall have been elected, and he shall not receive within that Period any other Emolument from the United States, or any of them.

Before he enters on the Execution of his Office, he shall take the following Oath or Affirmation:—"I do solemnly swear (or affirm) that I will faithfully execute the Office of President of the United States, and will to the best of my Ability, preserve, protect and defend the Constitution of the United States."

**Section. 2.**

The President shall be Commander in Chief of the Army and Navy of the United States, and of the Militia of the several States, when called into the actual Service of the United States; he may require the Opinion, in writing, of the principal Officer in each of the executive Departments, upon any Subject relating to the Duties of their respective Offices, and he shall have Power to grant Reprieves and Pardons for Offences against the United States, except in Cases of Impeachment.

He shall have Power, by and with the Advice and Consent of the Senate, to make Treaties, provided two thirds of the Senators present concur; and he shall nominate, and by and with the Advice and Consent of the Senate, shall appoint Ambassadors, other public Ministers and Consuls, Judges of the supreme Court, and all other Officers of the United States, whose Appointments are not herein otherwise provided for, and which shall be established by Law: but the Congress may by Law vest the Appointment of such inferior Officers, as they think proper, in the President alone, in the Courts of Law, or in the Heads of Departments.

The President shall have Power to fill up all Vacancies that may happen during the Recess of the Senate, by granting Commissions which shall expire at the End of their next Session.

**Section. 3.**

He shall from time to time give to the Congress Information of the State of the Union, and recommend to their Consideration such Measures as he shall judge necessary and expedient; he may, on extraordinary Occasions, convene both Houses, or either of them, and in Case of Disagreement between them, with Respect to the Time of Adjournment, he may adjourn them to such Time as he shall think proper; he shall receive Ambassadors and other public Ministers; he shall take Care that the Laws be faithfully executed, and shall Commission all the Officers of the United States.

**Section. 4.**

The President, Vice President and all civil Officers of the United States, shall be removed from Office on Impeachment for, and Conviction of, Treason, Bribery, or other high Crimes and Misdemeanors.

---

**Article III**

**Section. 1.**

The judicial Power of the United States, shall be vested in one supreme Court, and in such inferior Courts as the Congress may from time to time ordain and establish. The Judges, both of the supreme and inferior Courts, shall hold their Offices during good Behaviour, and shall, at stated Times, receive for their Services, a Compensation, which shall not be diminished during their Continuance in Office.

**Section. 2.**

The judicial Power shall extend to all Cases, in Law and Equity, arising under this Constitution, the Laws of the United States, and Treaties made, or which shall be made, under their Authority;—to all Cases affecting Ambassadors, other public Ministers and Consuls;—to all Cases of admiralty and maritime Jurisdiction;—to Controversies to which the United States shall be a Party;—to Controversies between two or more States;—between a State and Citizens of another State,—between Citizens of different States,—between Citizens of the same State claiming Lands under Grants of different States, and between a State, or the Citizens thereof, and foreign States, Citizens or Subjects.

In all Cases affecting Ambassadors, other public Ministers and Consuls, and those in which a State shall be Party, the supreme Court shall have original Jurisdiction. In all the other Cases before mentioned, the supreme Court shall have appellate Jurisdiction, both as to Law and Fact, with such Exceptions, and under such Regulations as the Congress shall make.

The Trial of all Crimes, except in Cases of Impeachment, shall be by Jury; and such Trial shall be held in the State where the said Crimes shall have been committed; but when not committed within any State, the Trial shall be at such Place or Places as the Congress may by Law have directed.

**Section. 3.**

Treason against the United States, shall consist only in levying War against them, or in adhering to their Enemies, giving them Aid and Comfort. No Person shall be convicted of Treason unless on the Testimony of two Witnesses to the same overt Act, or on Confession in open Court.

The Congress shall have Power to declare the Punishment of Treason, but no Attainder of Treason shall work Corruption of Blood, or Forfeiture except during the Life of the Person attainted.

## Article. IV

**Section. 1.**

Full Faith and Credit shall be given in each State to the public Acts, Records, and judicial Proceedings of every other State. And the Congress may by general Laws prescribe the Manner in which such Acts, Records and Proceedings shall be proved, and the Effect thereof.

**Section. 2.**

The Citizens of each State shall be entitled to all Privileges and Immunities of Citizens in the several States.

A Person charged in any State with Treason, Felony, or other Crime, who shall flee from Justice, and be found in another State, shall on Demand of the executive Authority of the State from which he fled, be delivered up, to be removed to the State having Jurisdiction of the Crime.

No Person held to Service or Labour in one State, under the Laws thereof, escaping into another, shall, in Consequence of any Law or Regulation therein, be discharged from such Service or Labour, but shall be delivered up on Claim of the Party to whom such Service or Labour may be due.

**Section. 3.**

New States may be admitted by the Congress into this Union; but no new State shall be formed or erected within the Jurisdiction of any other State; nor any State be formed by the Junction of two or more States, or Parts of States, without the Consent of the Legislatures of the States concerned as well as of the Congress.

The Congress shall have Power to dispose of and make all needful Rules and Regulations respecting the Territory or other Property belonging to the United States; and nothing in this Constitution shall be so construed as to Prejudice any Claims of the United States, or of any particular State.

**Section. 4.**

The United States shall guarantee to every State in this Union a Republican Form of Government, and shall protect each of them against Invasion; and on Application of the Legislature, or of the Executive (when the Legislature cannot be convened), against domestic Violence.

## Article. V

The Congress, whenever two thirds of both Houses shall deem it necessary, shall propose Amendments to this Constitution, or, on the Application of the Legislatures of two thirds of the several States, shall call a Convention for proposing Amendments, which, in either Case, shall be valid to all Intents and Purposes, as Part of this Constitution, when ratified by the Legislatures of three fourths of the several States, or by Conventions in three fourths thereof, as the one or the other Mode of Ratification may be proposed by the Congress; Provided that no Amendment which may be made prior to the Year One thousand eight hundred and eight shall in any Manner affect the first and fourth Clauses in the Ninth Section of the first Article; and that no State, without its Consent, shall be deprived of its equal Suffrage in the Senate.

### Article. VI

All Debts contracted and Engagements entered into, before the Adoption of this Constitution, shall be as valid against the United States under this Constitution, as under the Confederation.

This Constitution, and the Laws of the United States which shall be made in Pursuance thereof; and all Treaties made, or which shall be made, under the Authority of the United States, shall be the supreme Law of the Land; and the Judges in every State shall be bound thereby, any Thing in the Constitution or Laws of any State to the Contrary notwithstanding.

The Senators and Representatives before mentioned, and the Members of the several State Legislatures, and all executive and judicial Officers, both of the United States and of the several States, shall be bound by Oath or Affirmation, to support this Constitution; but no religious Test shall ever be required as a Qualification to any Office or public Trust under the United States.

---

### Article. VII

The Ratification of the Conventions of nine States, shall be sufficient for the Establishment of this Constitution between the States so ratifying the Same.

The Word, "the," being interlined between the seventh and eighth Lines of the first Page, The Word "Thirty" being partly written on an Erazure in the fifteenth Line of the first Page, The Words "is tried" being interlined between the thirty second and thirty third Lines of the first Page and the Word "the" being interlined between the forty third and forty fourth Lines of the second Page.

Attest William Jackson Secretary, done in Convention by the Unanimous Consent of the States present the Seventeenth Day of September in the Year of our Lord one thousand seven hundred and Eighty seven and of the Independance of the United States of America the Twelfth In witness whereof We have hereunto subscribed our Names, G°. Washington, *Presidt and deputy from Virginia*

**Delaware**
Geo: Read
Gunning Bedford jun
John Dickinson
Richard Bassett
Jaco: Broom

**Maryland**
James McHenry
Dan of St Thos. Jenifer
Danl. Carroll

**Virginia**
John Blair
James Madison Jr.

**North Carolina**
Wm. Blount
Richd. Dobbs Spaight
Hu Williamson

**South Carolina**
J. Rutledge
Charles Cotesworth Pinckney
Charles Pinckney
Pierce Butler

**Georgia**
William Few
Abr Baldwin

**New Hampshire**
John Langdon
Nicholas Gilman

**Massachusetts**
Nathaniel Gorham
Rufus King

**Connecticut**
Wm. Saml. Johnson
Roger Sherman

**New York**
Alexander Hamilton

**New Jersey**
Wil: Livingston
David Brearley
Wm. Paterson
Jona: Dayton

**Pensylvania**
B Franklin
Thomas Mifflin
Robt. Morris
Geo. Clymer
Thos. FitzSimons
Jared Ingersoll
James Wilson
Gouv Morris

## Enactment of the Bill of Rights of the United States of America (1791)

The first ten Amendments to the Constitution make up the Bill of Rights. Written by James Madison in response to calls from several states for greater constitutional protection for individual liberties, the Bill of Rights lists specific prohibitions on governmental power. The Virginia Declaration of Rights, written by George Mason, strongly influenced Madison.

One of the contention points between Federalists and Anti-Federalists was the Constitution's lack of a bill of rights that would place specific limits on government power.

Federalists argued that the Constitution did not need a bill of rights because the people and the states kept powers not explicitly given to the federal government.

Anti-Federalists held that a *bill of rights* was necessary to safeguard individual liberty.

Madison, then a member of the U.S. House of Representatives, went through the Constitution itself, making changes where he thought most appropriate.

Several Representatives, led by Roger Sherman, objected that Congress had no authority to change the wording of the Constitution. Therefore, Madison's changes were presented as a list of amendments that would follow Article VII.

The House approved 17 amendments. Of these 17, the Senate approved 12. Those 12 were sent to the states for approval in August of 1789. Of those 12 proposed amendments, 10 were quickly ratified. Virginia's legislature became the last to ratify the Amendments on December 15, 1791. These Amendments are the Bill of Rights.

The Bill of Rights is a list of limits on government power. For example, what the Founders saw as the natural right of individuals to speak and worship freely was protected by the First Amendment's prohibitions on Congress from making laws establishing a religion or abridging freedom of speech.

Another example is the natural right to be free from the government's unreasonable intrusion in one's home was safeguarded by the Fourth Amendment's warrant requirements.

Other precursors to the Bill of Rights include English documents such as the Magna Carta[1], the Petition of Rights, the English Bill of Rights, and the Massachusetts Body of Liberties.

The Magna Carta illustrates Compact Theory[1] as well as initial strides toward limited government. Its provisions address individual rights and political rights. Latin for "Great Charter," the Magna Carta was written by Barons in Runnymede, England, and forced on the King.

Although the protections were generally limited to the prerogatives of the Barons, the Magna Carta embodied the general principle that the King accepted limitations on his rule. These included the fundamental acknowledgment that the king was not above the law.

Included in the Magna Carta are protections for the English church, petitioning the king, freedom from the forced quarter of troops and unreasonable searches, due process and fair trial protections, and freedom from excessive fines. These protections can be found in the First, Third, Fourth, Fifth, Sixth, and Eighth Amendments to the Constitution.

The Magna Carta is the oldest compact in England. The Mayflower Compact, the Fundamental Orders of Connecticut, and the Albany Plan are examples from the American colonies.

The Articles of Confederation was a compact among the states, and the Constitution creates a compact based on a federal system between the national government, state governments, and the people. The Hayne-Webster Debate focused on the compact created by the Constitution.

---

[1] Philosophers including Thomas Hobbes, John Locke, and Jean-Jacques Rousseau theorized that peoples' condition in a "state of nature" (that is, outside of society) is one of freedom, but that freedom inevitably degrades into war, chaos, or debilitating competition without the benefit of a system of laws and government. They reasoned, therefore, that for their happiness, individuals willingly trade some of their natural freedom in exchange for the protections provided by the government.

## The Bill of Rights: Amendments I–X

### Amendment I

Congress shall make no law respecting an establishment of religion, or prohibiting the free exercise thereof; or abridging the freedom of speech, or of the press; or the right of the people peaceably to assemble, and to petition the government for a redress of grievances.

### Amendment II

A well regulated militia, being necessary to the security of a free state, the right of the people to keep and bear arms, shall not be infringed.

### Amendment III

No soldier shall, in time of peace be quartered in any house, without the consent of the owner, nor in time of war, but in a manner to be prescribed by law.

### Amendment IV

The right of the people to be secure in their persons, houses, papers, and effects, against unreasonable searches and seizures, shall not be violated, and no warrants shall issue, but upon probable cause, supported by oath or affirmation, and particularly describing the place to be searched, and the persons or things to be seized.

### Amendment V

No person shall be held to answer for a capital, or otherwise infamous crime, unless on a presentment or indictment of a grand jury, except in cases arising in the land or naval forces, or in the militia, when in actual service in time of war or public danger; nor shall any person be subject for the same offense to be twice put in jeopardy of life or limb; nor shall be compelled in any criminal case to be a witness against himself, nor be deprived of life, liberty, or property, without due process of law; nor shall private property be taken for public use, without just compensation.

### Amendment VI

In all criminal prosecutions, the accused shall enjoy the right to a speedy and public trial, by an impartial jury of the state and district wherein the crime shall have been committed, which district shall have been previously ascertained by law, and to be informed of the nature and cause of the accusation; to be confronted with the witnesses against him; to have compulsory process for obtaining witnesses in his favor, and to have the assistance of counsel for his defense.

### Amendment VII

In suits at common law, where the value in controversy shall exceed twenty dollars, the right of trial by jury shall be preserved, and no fact tried by a jury, shall be otherwise reexamined in any court of the United States, than according to the rules of the common law.

### Amendment VIII

Excessive bail shall not be required, nor excessive fines imposed, nor cruel and unusual punishments inflicted.

### Amendment IX

The enumeration in the Constitution, of certain rights, shall not be construed to deny or disparage others retained by the people.

### Amendment X

The powers not delegated to the United States by the Constitution, nor prohibited by it to the states, are reserved to the states respectively, or to the people.

## Constitutional Amendments XI–XXVII

### AMENDMENT XI

*Passed by Congress March 4, 1794. Ratified February 7, 1795.*

Note: Article III, section 2, of the Constitution was modified by amendment 11.

The Judicial power of the United States shall not be construed to extend to any suit in law or equity, commenced or prosecuted against one of the United States by Citizens of another State, or by Citizens or Subjects of any Foreign State.

---

### AMENDMENT XII

*Passed by Congress December 9, 1803. Ratified June 15, 1804.*

Note: A portion of Article II, section 1 of the Constitution was superseded by the 12th amendment.

The Electors shall meet in their respective states and vote by ballot for President and Vice-President, one of whom, at least, shall not be an inhabitant of the same state with themselves; they shall name in their ballots the person voted for as President, and in distinct ballots the person voted for as Vice-President, and they shall make distinct lists of all persons voted for as President, and of all persons voted for as Vice-President, and of the number of votes for each, which lists they shall sign and certify, and transmit sealed to the seat of the government of the United States, directed to the President of the Senate; -- the President of the Senate shall, in the presence of the Senate and House of Representatives, open all the certificates and the votes shall then be counted; -- The person having the greatest number of votes for President, shall be the President, if such number be a majority of the whole number of Electors appointed; and if no person have such majority, then from the persons having the highest numbers not exceeding three on the list of those voted for as President, the House of Representatives shall choose immediately, by ballot, the President. But in choosing the President, the votes shall be taken by states, the representation from each state having one vote; a quorum for this purpose shall consist of a member or members from two-thirds of the states, and a majority of all the states shall be necessary to a choice. [And if the House of Representatives shall not choose a President whenever the right of choice shall devolve upon them, before the fourth day of March next following, then the Vice-President shall act as President, as in case of the death or other constitutional disability of the President. --]* The person having the greatest number of votes as Vice-President, shall be the Vice-President, if such number be a majority of the whole number of Electors appointed, and if no person have a majority, then from the two highest numbers on the list, the Senate shall choose the Vice-President; a quorum for the purpose shall consist of two-thirds of the whole number of Senators, and a majority of the whole number shall be necessary to a choice. But no person constitutionally ineligible to the office of President shall be eligible to that of Vice-President of the United States.

*Superseded by section 3 of the 20th Amendment.

## AMENDMENT XIII

*Passed by Congress January 31, 1865. Ratified December 6, 1865.*

**Note**: A portion of Article IV, section 2, of the Constitution was superseded by the 13th amendment.

**Section 1.**
Neither slavery nor involuntary servitude, except as a punishment for crime whereof the party shall have been duly convicted, shall exist within the United States, or any place subject to their jurisdiction.

**Section 2.**
Congress shall have power to enforce this article by appropriate legislation.

---

## AMENDMENT XIV

*Passed by Congress June 13, 1866. Ratified July 9, 1868.*

**Note**: Article I, section 2, of the Constitution was modified by section 2 of the 14th amendment.

**Section 1.**
All persons born or naturalized in the United States, and subject to the jurisdiction thereof, are citizens of the United States and of the State wherein they reside. No State shall make or enforce any law which shall abridge the privileges or immunities of citizens of the United States; nor shall any State deprive any person of life, liberty, or property, without due process of law; nor deny to any person within its jurisdiction the equal protection of the laws.

**Section 2.**
Representatives shall be apportioned among the several States according to their respective numbers, counting the whole number of persons in each State, excluding Indians not taxed. But when the right to vote at any election for the choice of electors for President and Vice-President of the United States, Representatives in Congress, the Executive and Judicial officers of a State, or the members of the Legislature thereof, is denied to any of the male inhabitants of such State, being twenty-one years of age,* and citizens of the United States, or in any way abridged, except for participation in rebellion, or other crime, the basis of representation therein shall be reduced in the proportion which the number of such male citizens shall bear to the whole number of male citizens twenty-one years of age in such State.

**Section 3.**
No person shall be a Senator or Representative in Congress, or elector of President and Vice-President, or hold any office, civil or military, under the United States, or under any State, who, having previously taken an oath, as a member of Congress, or as an officer of the United States, or as a member of any State legislature, or as an executive or judicial officer of any State, to support the Constitution of the United States, shall have engaged in insurrection or rebellion against the same, or given aid or comfort to the enemies thereof. But Congress may by a vote of two-thirds of each House, remove such disability.

**Section 4.**

The validity of the public debt of the United States, authorized by law, including debts incurred for payment of pensions and bounties for services in suppressing insurrection or rebellion, shall not be questioned. But neither the United States nor any State shall assume or pay any debt or obligation incurred in aid of insurrection or rebellion against the United States, or any claim for the loss or emancipation of any slave; but all such debts, obligations and claims shall be held illegal and void.

**Section 5.**

The Congress shall have the power to enforce, by appropriate legislation, the provisions of this article.

*\*Changed by section 1 of the 26th Amendment.*

## AMENDMENT XV

*Passed by Congress February 26, 1869. Ratified February 3, 1870.*

**Section 1.**

The right of citizens of the United States to vote shall not be denied or abridged by the United States or by any State on account of race, color, or previous condition of servitude.

**Section 2.**

The Congress shall have the power to enforce this article by appropriate legislation.

## AMENDMENT XVI

*Passed by Congress July 2, 1909. Ratified February 3, 1913.*

**Note**: Article I, section 9, of the Constitution was modified by amendment 16.

The Congress shall have power to lay and collect taxes on incomes, from whatever source derived, without apportionment among the several States, and without regard to any census or enumeration.

## AMENDMENT XVII

*Passed by Congress May 13, 1912. Ratified April 8, 1913.*

**Note**: Article I, section 3, of the Constitution was modified by the 17th Amendment.

The Senate of the United States shall be composed of two Senators from each State, elected by the people thereof, for six years; and each Senator shall have one vote. The electors in each State shall have the qualifications requisite for electors of the most numerous branch of the State legislatures.

When vacancies happen in the representation of any State in the Senate, the executive authority of such State shall issue writs of election to fill such vacancies: *Provided*, That the legislature of any State may empower the executive thereof to make temporary appointments until the people fill the vacancies by election as the legislature may direct.

This amendment shall not be so construed as to affect the election or term of any Senator chosen before it becomes valid as part of the Constitution.

## AMENDMENT XVIII

*Passed by Congress December 18, 1917. Ratified January 16, 1919. Repealed by Amendment 21.*

**Section 1.**

After one year from the ratification of this article the manufacture, sale, or transportation of intoxicating liquors within, the importation thereof into, or the exportation thereof from the United States and all territory subject to the jurisdiction thereof for beverage purposes is hereby prohibited.

**Section 2.**

The Congress and the several States shall have concurrent power to enforce this article by appropriate legislation.

**Section 3.**

This article shall be inoperative unless it shall have been ratified as an amendment to the Constitution by the legislatures of the several States, as provided in the Constitution, within seven years from the date of the submission hereof to the States by the Congress.

## AMENDMENT XIX

*Passed by Congress June 4, 1919. Ratified August 18, 1920.*

The right of citizens of the United States to vote shall not be denied or abridged by the United States or by any State on account of sex.

Congress shall have power to enforce this article by appropriate legislation.

## AMENDMENT XX

*Passed by Congress March 2, 1932. Ratified January 23, 1933.*

**Note**: Article I, section 4, of the Constitution was modified by section 2 of this Amendment. In addition, a portion of the 12th Amendment was superseded by section 3.

**Section 1.**
The terms of the President and the Vice President shall end at noon on the 20th day of January, and the terms of Senators and Representatives at noon on the 3d day of January, of the years in which such terms would have ended if this article had not been ratified; and the terms of their successors shall then begin.

**Section 2.**
The Congress shall assemble at least once in every year, and such meeting shall begin at noon on the 3d day of January, unless they shall by law appoint a different day.

## Section 3.

If, at the time fixed for the beginning of the term of the President, the President elect shall have died, the Vice President elect shall become President. If a President shall not have been chosen before the time fixed for the beginning of his term, or if the President elect shall have failed to qualify, then the Vice President elect shall act as President until a President shall have qualified; and the Congress may by law provide for the case wherein neither a President elect nor a Vice President elect shall have qualified, declaring who shall then act as President, or the manner in which one who is to act shall be selected, and such person shall act accordingly until a President or Vice President shall have qualified.

## Section 4.

The Congress may by law provide for the case of the death of any of the persons from whom the House of Representatives may choose a President whenever the right of choice shall have devolved upon them, and for the case of the death of any of the persons from whom the Senate may choose a Vice President whenever the right of choice shall have devolved upon them.

## Section 5.

Sections 1 and 2 shall take effect on the 15th day of October following the ratification of this article.

## Section 6.

This article shall be inoperative unless it shall have been ratified as an amendment to the Constitution by the legislatures of three-fourths of the several States within seven years from the date of its submission.

## AMENDMENT XXI

*Passed by Congress February 20, 1933. Ratified December 5, 1933.*

## Section 1.

The eighteenth article of amendment to the Constitution of the United States is hereby repealed.

## Section 2.

The transportation or importation into any State, Territory, or possession of the United States for delivery or use therein of intoxicating liquors, in violation of the laws thereof, is hereby prohibited.

## Section 3.

This article shall be inoperative unless it shall have been ratified as an amendment to the Constitution by conventions in the several States, as provided in the Constitution, within seven years from the date of the submission hereof to the States by the Congress.

## AMENDMENT XXII

*Passed by Congress March 21, 1947. Ratified February 27, 1951.*

**Section 1.**
No person shall be elected to the office of the President more than twice, and no person who has held the office of President, or acted as President, for more than two years of a term to which some other person was elected President shall be elected to the office of the President more than once. But this Article shall not apply to any person holding the office of President when this Article was proposed by the Congress, and shall not prevent any person who may be holding the office of President, or acting as President, during the term within which this Article becomes operative from holding the office of President or acting as President during the remainder of such term.

**Section 2.**
This article shall be inoperative unless it shall have been ratified as an amendment to the Constitution by the legislatures of three-fourths of the several States within seven years from the date of its submission to the States by the Congress.

---

## AMENDMENT XXIII

*Passed by Congress June 16, 1960. Ratified March 29, 1961.*

**Section 1.**
The District constituting the seat of Government of the United States shall appoint in such manner as the Congress may direct:

A number of electors of President and Vice President equal to the whole number of Senators and Representatives in Congress to which the District would be entitled if it were a State, but in no event more than the least populous State; they shall be in addition to those appointed by the States, but they shall be considered, for the purposes of the election of President and Vice President, to be electors appointed by a State; and they shall meet in the District and perform such duties as provided by the twelfth article of amendment.

**Section 2.**
The Congress shall have power to enforce this article by appropriate legislation.

---

## AMENDMENT XXIV

*Passed by Congress August 27, 1962. Ratified January 23, 1964.*

**Section 1.**
The right of citizens of the United States to vote in any primary or other election for President or Vice President, for electors for President or Vice President, or for Senator or Representative in Congress, shall not be denied or abridged by the United States or any State by reason of failure to pay any poll tax or other tax.

**Section 2.**
The Congress shall have power to enforce this article by appropriate legislation.

---

## AMENDMENT XXV

*Passed by Congress July 6, 1965. Ratified February 10, 1967.*

**Note**: Article II, section 1, of the Constitution was affected by the 25th amendment.

**Section 1.**
In case of the removal of the President from office or of his death or resignation, the Vice President shall become President.

**Section 2.**
Whenever there is a vacancy in the office of the Vice President, the President shall nominate a Vice President who shall take office upon confirmation by a majority vote of both Houses of Congress.

**Section 3.**
Whenever the President transmits to the President pro tempore of the Senate and the Speaker of the House of Representatives his written declaration that he is unable to discharge the powers and duties of his office, and until he transmits to them a written declaration to the contrary, such powers and duties shall be discharged by the Vice President as Acting President.

**Section 4.**
Whenever the Vice President and a majority of either the principal officers of the executive departments or of such other body as Congress may by law provide, transmit to the President pro tempore of the Senate and the Speaker of the House of Representatives their written declaration that the President is unable to discharge the powers and duties of his office, the Vice President shall immediately assume the powers and duties of the office as Acting President.

Thereafter, when the President transmits to the President pro tempore of the Senate and the Speaker of the House of Representatives his written declaration that no inability exists, he shall resume the powers and duties of his office unless the Vice President and a majority of either the principal officers of the executive department or of such other body as Congress may by law provide, transmit within four days to the President pro tempore of the Senate and the Speaker of the House of Representatives their written declaration that the President is unable to discharge the powers and duties of his office. Thereupon Congress shall decide the issue, assembling within forty-eight hours for that purpose if not in session. If the Congress, within twenty-one days after receipt of the latter written declaration, or, if Congress is not in session, within twenty-one days after Congress is required to assemble, determines by two-thirds vote of both Houses that the President is unable to discharge the powers and duties of his office, the Vice President shall continue to discharge the same as Acting President; otherwise, the President shall resume the powers and duties of his office.

## AMENDMENT XXVI

*Passed by Congress March 23, 1971. Ratified July 1, 1971.*

**Note**: Amendment 14, section 2, of the Constitution was modified by section 1 of the 26th amendment.

**Section 1.**
The right of citizens of the United States, who are eighteen years of age or older, to vote shall not be denied or abridged by the United States or by any State on account of age.

**Section 2.**
The Congress shall have power to enforce this article by appropriate legislation.

---

## AMENDMENT XXVII

*Originally proposed Sept. 25, 1789. Ratified May 7, 1992.*

No law, varying the compensation for the services of the Senators and Representatives, shall take effect, until an election of Representatives shall have intervened

## States' Rights Under the U.S. Constitution

### Selective incorporation under the 14th Amendment

The U.S. Constitution has Articles and Amendments that established constitutional rights.

The provisions in the Bill of Rights (i.e., the first ten Amendments to the Constitution) were initially binding upon only the federal government.

In time, most of these provisions became binding upon the states through *selective incorporation* into the *due process clause* of the 14th Amendment (i.e., reverse incorporation).

When a provision is made binding on a state, a state can no longer restrict the rights guaranteed in that provision.

The 1st Amendment guarantees the freedoms of speech, press, religion, and assembly.

The 5th Amendment protects the right to grand jury proceedings in federal criminal cases.

The 6th Amendment guarantees a right to confront witnesses (i.e., Confrontation Clause).

The right to confront witnesses was not *selectively incorporated* into the due process clause of the 14th Amendment and is not binding upon the states.

Therefore, persons involved in state criminal proceedings as a defendant have no federal constitutional right to grand jury proceedings.

Whether an individual has a right to a grand jury becomes a question of state law.

The 10th Amendment, which is part of the Bill of Rights, was ratified on December 15, 1791. It states the Constitution's principle of federalism by providing that powers not granted to the federal government by the Constitution, nor prohibited to the States, are reserved to the States or the people.

### Federalism in the United States

Federalism in the United States is the evolving relationship between state governments and the federal government.

The American government has evolved from a system of dual federalism to associative federalism.

In "Federalist No. 46," James Madison wrote that the states and national government "are in fact but different agents and trustees of the people, constituted with different powers."

Alexander Hamilton, in "Federalist No. 28," suggested that both levels of government would exercise authority to the citizens' benefit: "If their [the peoples'] rights are invaded by either, they can make use of the other as the instrument of redress."[3]

Because the states were preexisting political entities, the U.S. Constitution did not need to define or explain federalism in one section, but it often mentions the rights and responsibilities of state governments and state officials in relation to the federal government.

The federal government has certain *express powers* (also called *enumerated powers*), which are powers spelled out in the Constitution, including the right to levy taxes, declare war, and regulate interstate and foreign commerce.

Also, the *Necessary and Proper Clause* gives the federal government the *implied power* to pass any law "necessary and proper" to execute its express powers.

Enumerated powers of the Federal Government are contained in Article I, Section 8 of the U.S. Constitution.

Other powers—the *reserved powers*—are reserved to the people or the states under the 10th Amendment. The Supreme Court decision significantly expanded the power delegated to the federal government in *McCulloch v. Maryland* (1819) and the 13th, 14th and 15th, Amendments to the Constitution following the Civil War.

## *Law Essentials* series

| | |
|---|---|
| Constitutional Law | Criminal Law and Criminal Procedure |
| Contracts | Business Associations |
| Evidence | Conflict of Laws |
| Real Property | Family Law |
| Torts | Secured Transactions |
| Civil Procedure | Trusts and Estates |

**Visit our Amazon store**

*Comprehensive Glossary of Legal Terms*

Over 2,100 essential legal terms defined and explained. An excellent reference source for law students, practitioners and readers seeking an understanding of legal vocabulary and its application.

*Landmark U.S. Supreme Court Cases: Essential Summaries*

Learn important constitutional cases that shaped American law. Understand how the evolving needs of society intersect with the U.S. Constitution. Short summaries of seminal Supreme Court cases focused on issues and holdings.

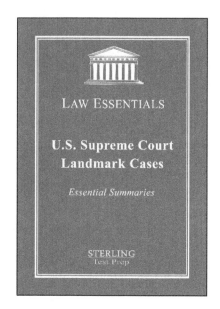

**Visit our Amazon store**

# Frank J. Addivinola, Ph.D., J.D., L.LM., MBA

The lead author and chief editor of this preparation guide is Dr. Frank Addivinola. With his outstanding education, professional training, legal and business experience, and university teaching, Dr. Addivinola lent his expertise to develop this book.

Attorney Frank Addivinola is admitted to practice law in several jurisdictions. He has served as an academic advisor and mentor for students and practitioners.

Dr. Addivinola holds an undergraduate degree from Williams College. He completed his Masters at Harvard University, Masters in Biotechnology at Johns Hopkins University, Masters in Technology Management and MBA at the University of Maryland University College, J.D. and L.LM. from Suffolk University, and Ph.D. in Law and Public Policy from Northeastern University.

During his extensive teaching career, Dr. Addivinola taught university courses in Introduction to Law and developed law coursebooks. He received several awards for community service, research, and presentations.

Printed in France by Amazon
Brétigny-sur-Orge, FR

14356009R00092